A MARRIAGE WITH CELIBATES

A MARRIAGE WITH CELIBATES

—∞∞—

Virginia Finn: A Memoir

After 30 years as a prominent lay minister, Virginia Finn shares how she championed for the lay people and uncovers how the Church stifled the faith and fidelity of the people in the pews.

First paperback edition 2017

Finn, Virginia
ISBN-13: 9781541115101
ISBN-10: 1541115104

Printed by CreateSpace.

Available from Amazon, presspreach.com, and other retail outlets.
Available on Kindle.

Cover Design by Dorit Tabak
www.tabakdesign.com

Thanks Be To God

I thank my readers and editors Tierney Fitzmartin, Pamela Magahiz,
William Barry, Jane Olin, and Linda Karten
for their patience and curiosity.

I pray for the priests, bishops, and Weston alumni
that I have worked with over the years
and are still fighting for change in our Church.

I cherish my dear friends from the Vineyard Community
and the Berkshires.

I am so very grateful for my neighbors in South Lee,
who are my guardian angels.

I thank my daughter, Tierney, for her unwavering support and
insistence that I finish the book.

*I dedicate this to Tara Virginia,
my youngest grandchild, who many years ago showed me
the contemplative joy to be found in mud puddles.*

PREFACE

"Are you Jewish?"

If you were asked that question and answered in the affirmative, you might then be asked. "Are you Orthodox, Conservative, or Reform?"

"Are you Protestant?"

If asked that and you answered in the affirmative, you might then hear a further inquiry. "Are you Presbyterian, Methodist, Episcopalian, Unitarian, or Quaker? Do you belong to the United Church of Christ?"

"Are you a Catholic?"

When that is asked of me, there is no follow-up inquiry once I reply in the affirmative. Sometimes I wonder if the questioner thinks I pray rosary beads everyday. Other assumptions could be drawn. Cradle Catholic, parochial school, Catholic college, follows all the demands from the Vatican. Only the first of those is true. A quick glance at my left hand reveals tell-tale signs of identity; married so not a nun, woman so not a priest.

The shame is that people who are not Catholic, and even many who are, are unaware of the abundant variety of people in the Roman Catholic fold.

Pope Francis is a brave new pope. He is reaching out to the lay people; he is listening to God's people. By serving the people he is strengthening the Church. He is removing the money changers from Rome and cleaning house. Still, the matters of ordaining women and the marrying of priests are still too far down the road to Damascus.

The Catholic Church has 226 cardinals, 5,237 bishops, 415,792 priests–and one billion lay people. The clergy makes up less than one percent of the Catholic community. However, in the Church and in the media, the rest of us are often reduced to an "issue." Divorce, birth control, abortion, homosexuality, lapsed. I don't think anyone likes being an 'issue.'

I am a Catholic layperson with a rich personal life. I was married for 49 years, raised four children and savor my five grandchildren. I worked in the Church as a spiritual director, educator, Eucharistic minister, and served in hospitals and on college campuses. I have spoken on behalf of the church in religious publications, as well as on the radio and television. If the Church wants to survive and flourish, the clergy need to listen to our voices—the 99%.

The formation of the spirit within believers, ordained and lay people, is intriguing but complicated as well. For many cradle Catholics it's been a lifelong experience. At times, it feels like a voyage on high seas with winds balanced by occasions in tranquil lagoons. Just like the variety of animals on the famous ark, we have a variety of people– rebellious radicals, curators of dinosaurs, conniving pirates, valiant loyalists, and many who frequently jump ship. But the ship creaks on and manages to stay afloat. For the time being.

In the crowd of valiant loyalists I can be found. I found that a transformation of my spirit within self, which happened within a church that was transforming itself. I am not alone in this process. Laywomen and laymen, married or celibate, young or hopeful, old or wise, leaders, priests, sisters, or bishops are all on the journey. And we need to go together.

When I first began my career in 1964, the Church did not really use the term "lay minister." Even today, the word 'lay' is a fluid term, just like God's spirit and Her people. In this memoir, I use 'lay people' to describe Catholics and 'lay ministers' to describe those Catholics who volunteer or work for the Church.

The National Association of Lay Ministry highlights five areas of ministry: Pastoral Associates and Parish Life Coordinators, Directors of Liturgy, Catechetical Leaders, Youth Ministry Directors, and Directors of Musical Ministry. In 1979 I was the Chairwoman of the NALM and there 500 members. Today there are 2,000. This is a testament to the calling the Catholic lay people have to ministry.

INTRODUCTION

"You ate no lunch," my mother would entreat.
"Mon Dieu feeds me," Pépère would respond.
"You must have been frozen."
"Mon Dieu keeps me warm."
"You must have been lonely."
"Mon Dieu keeps me company."

I grew up in an ethnically rich town dominated by textile mills, next to the Connecticut River in Massachusetts. Easthampton was dominated by five Catholic churches, including a Polish, a French, and an Irish. After school I often made a visit to Notre Dame, because it was on the way home and my grandfather would be there. My family 'belonged' to Immaculate Conception, even though it was a 45-minute walk from my house. That was my father's church, and in those days you attended mass at the husband's church.

The French church was open all day, Pepere let himself be drawn to God. I would sit next to him quietly and we would keep God company. Then I would freely walk around the church. I might light a candle by Mary's altar, walk along the walls of the nave to follow the Stations of the Cross, or say a decade of the rosary. Then my grandfather and I would walk home, where my mother would express her worrying, even before we ate supper, that Pepere was gone all day.

My identity from the start was problematic. On March 17th I was born in the regional hospital in western Massachusetts. At seven a.m., my mother and father agreed my Christian name was Patricia in honor of the saint; 12 hours later, my Christian name was changed to Virginia. This name change was the deed of my father, a mailman. As he went from house to house that day, he was told by everyone in town to name me after St. Patrick. Being Irish, he rebelled.

My mother, Blanche Bernadette Bouthillette, came from a particularly devout family. Every New Year's Day, I went with my parents to Pepere's house, along with my mother's twelve brothers and sisters, and my cousins. We would kneel on the large braided rug and receive our blessings from Pepere. I was my parents' only child. My father was so proud when I was accepted into the University of Massachusetts in 1948. Tommy had wanted to attend college, but his family had pressured him to get a job instead. My mother went to work in a toothbrush factory when she was fourteen and that's where she learned English. Mother would only hear of my attending college if I lived at home. Blanche didn't want to be alone with Tommy. He drank.

At the end of my junior year in high school I confronted my father about the drinking. For the first time in history, my high school was to be in a qualifying game for the state championship. After school, I rushed home to get the money I had saved up from working, to buy tickets for the game and for the bus that my friends and I would take all the way across the state for the big game. I raced up the stairs to my bedroom. The mattress was shoved halfway off the bed. The drawers spilled out. Clothes off the hangers in the closet. I dashed back downstairs and found my father, drunk, sitting on the sofa.

I scratched my hand across his face. "You stole my money. I hate you! I hate you!"

"You're right, I deserve it. I deserve it," he mumbled.

With the long scar on his face, Daddy didn't leave the duplex for days, but I went to confession at nearby Notre Dame, where a priest who had been a Navy chaplain was assigned temporarily. I could not risk going to the church where my family belonged. In the confessional I told the priest about Daddy, his dishonorable discharge, his drinking, and his stealing from me, as well as my attacking him. After I said the Act of Contrition, he dismissed me. I said, "But you haven't given me my penance."

"No, I haven't, because there is no sin. You have a terrible situation. I'll pray for you. God's blessing. And don't forget, God loves you."

When I left the church, I couldn't believe what had happened. Who had ever heard of going to confession and not getting a penance? He seemed to feel what I felt. My mother worked two jobs, walking three miles to the mill at seven in the morning. She worked Friday evening and all day Saturday in a dress shop. She cooked on Sunday but during the week, after I did the dishes, she was asleep on the sofa with the daily paper over her face.

My father didn't work much, sometimes not at all, but he read constantly and talked to me about his books. Still, I often felt like I had no mother or father, but I now knew I had God to take their place and take care of me. That blessing would determine my whole life.

The summer before I started college, two more blessings came to me. Blanche told Tommy that if he continued to drink, she would move out too. He stopped. Then I met George. Tall, with a mass of curly black hair and eyes as dark as midnight, he was from Northampton, the small college town right next door. We courted all through college. He was at Brown University and on the weekends we would go out to dance the fox-trot and listen to Duke Ellington.

We were married February 27, 1954 at Immaculate Conception and our reception was held at the elegant Hotel Northampton. George wanted to go to Florida for our honeymoon, but I had romantic dreams of skiing and sipping cocoa in Quebec. As would often happen over the course of our forty-nine years together, George supported my dream, but we did freeze in Canada.

At the beginning of our marriage, there was an unseen presence in our bedroom–the Church. We were trying to obey the Church's ban on birth control and, like many couples at the time, we were following the rhythm method. And like many others, our family began to grow. Leslie was born in 1955. Katherine and Pamela arrived eighteen months later. The twins were born six-weeks premature. After having three babies in less than two years, we prayed for the strength to obey the Church.

We discovered that the intense emotional intimacy of a partnership often leads to wonderful romantic intimacy. In our marriage, however, with the Church present in our bedroom, romance became the enemy. We gave up and focused instead on the responsibilities of raising a family, and our marriage began to crumble.

Over the next eight years, I had five miscarriages. At the beginning of my sixth pregnancy, the doctor wisely put me on bed rest. Tierney was born in 1963, another beautiful baby girl. After obeying the Church for eighteen years, we decided to start using birth control.

Four months after Tierney arrived, George lost his job and I returned to teaching full-time. George became a stay-at-home dad, a man ahead of the times, managing our brood. It was challenging for him. His personality, once spirited and excitable turned temperamental and irritable.

Eventually, George secured a position with a cutlery manufacturer in New Hampshire. Although this meant our family was being uprooted, it was actually a relief for me. I was finally leaving the town I had grown up in and was hopeful that a change of scenery would be good for everyone.

1

THE SEMINARY

Keene, New Hampshire, 1964

"There are seventy-five men, and you will be the only woman?"

"Yes."

"Are you the first woman to work there?"

" I think so. Well, I'm definitely the first woman to teach there."

"Aren't you petrified?"

"No, no. These are just priests and seminarians. What can go wrong?"

As I sat at my patio table with Martha, each of us taking a much needed break from our housework and children, I realized how much I had come to enjoy my new friend's company and how fortunate I was to have Martha as a neighbor. But she clearly had concerns about my latest venture. I couldn't worry too much about it. I needed to prepare my curriculum and figure out who was going to handle the kids while I was at work.

In Keene, George was happier once he got back to work, and the city environment provided more stimulation for both of us. Together we became active in our local parish and were fortunate to be introduced to the Church's new teachings on the Second Vatican Council or Vatican II. The bishop of our diocese firmly instructed his priests to inform their parishes about the changes prescribed by Vatican II.

George and I were invited to serve on a city ecumenical committee in the spirit of the Council. As I saw it, the central call of Vatican II was reform, collegiality, and mission. Communion rails no longer isolated priests from their parishioners, and parishioners had the choice of receiving Communion on the tongue or in the palm of their hand. Now the priests and people were able to fully embrace Sunday services.

While serving on the ecumenical committee, I made friends with Connie Daniels, who was grieving the loss of her son Jonathan, an Episcopal seminarian, who was shot and died helping African-Americans gain their civil rights in the South. We joined others in sending food and clothes to the church where Connie's son had worked before he was killed. George and I also met the dean of a nearby seminary, Queen of Peace. Like a few of the other parishioners, we welcomed Fr. Gilbert over to the house for Sunday dinner. We were surprised, however, when the doorbell rang on a week night in mid-August. Leslie answered the door and joyfully announced: "Mom, Dad, Fr. Gilbert is here!"

There was a crisis at the Queen of Peace, Gilbert explained. The faculty was short by one professor and the fall semester started in two weeks. The rector of the seminary, Fr. Evan, had hired a professor from a nearby Catholic college to teach a homiletics class. However, the priest had been in a serious car accident and would be unable to teach for at least the semester. As George offered him a beer, Gilbert pulled out a chair for me at the kitchen table. He took a sip of beer and over the rim of the glass eyed us both.

"Ginny, you'd be just perfect to join our faculty as the professor of preaching."

"But, we just moved here. I have the girls and Tierney is a baby."

"It's only part-time," pleaded Gilbert.

"But I teach English."

"You're always too modest," George said taking my hand. "You took writing and drama courses in college. You have a Master's in Education. And we could use the extra money."

"Just say you're willing to talk to the rector," Gilbert urged. "You don't have to decide now."

I gave Gilbert my answer before the end of the week and soon began teaching at the Queen of Peace Seminary.

Early on a Saturday before I was to start at the seminary, I went to meet Rector Evan. A man in his fifties, with thin grey hair and gold-rimmed glasses, he genially gave me the grand tour. The grounds were breathtaking: a small orchard of lush trees overflowing with nearly ripe apples; rolling lawns with oak trees for shade; and modern wooden benches where one could take in magnificent views of Mount Monadnock. In an adjacent field, the seminarians were playing ball. Their white habits fluttering in the breeze, they reminded me of angels. It was peaceful, quiet.

The main building was a huge old estate house, sparsely appointed with second-hand furniture. Gilbert explained, "It may be shabby to you Ginny, but we keep it intentionally modest to reflect the simplicity of our vow of poverty. We were on a first name basis at Queen of Peace; even the seminarians were permitted to address the priests by their first names. But this presented a problem in my case. Fortunately, Gilbert had come up with a solution. "The priests may call you 'Ginny,' but the seminarians will have to call you 'Mrs. Finn,'" he announced. *Am I supposed to thank him for assigning me an identity?*

"She is your mother."

The provincial towered over the lectern and pointed his index finger at the seminarians. "Respect Mrs. Finn as much as you respect your own mother. Never consider her as anything other than your mother."

Yet another identity! I was hired to be their professor. I already have four children and I love each one! I don't need fifty more. But this was the superior of the ecclesiastical province introducing me at the inaugural liturgy of the new school year. Not the time for a discussion.

The service went quickly, or perhaps it felt that way as I tried to establish whom everybody was. The placement of everyone in the small chapel helped. A "provincial" is actually a priest who is the head of an entire province. Standing next to him at the altar was Rector Evan, and beside him Fr. Gilbert. In the two front pews sat the faculty, sitting in order from eldest to youngest, with "Mrs. Finn" at the end. Behind us were the rows of student seminarians, some of them at least the same as their new "mother." At one point I was nudged by the professor next to me to proceed to the altar with all the other men in the first two rows. The provincial gave us a directive and I dutifully followed the other faculty members with their response.

As soon as the Mass ended, I hurried over to Gilbert.

"What happened up at the altar? Everything went so quickly."

"You took the oath."

"What oath?" I tried to slow him down as we proceeded to the rectory for an elaborate luncheon.

"It is the 'Oath Against Modernism.' Rome insists on it."

"But I don't know if I am against modernism. Isn't Vatican II about becoming more modern?"

"It's just a formality. If you had had any formal Catholic education, you'd understand. Don't worry about it."

On the first day of classes I realized how hard the students and I would need to work. I seemed to be the right person to teach preaching. A few of the younger students had just arrived from Ireland and seemed unsteady, even in this protective environment. Others were older, including a veteran of the Korean War, and could be intimidating. They all were book-smart and knew their scriptures.

Many of the students were not comfortable with oral presentations, so I began by having everyone, including myself, read poetry aloud. Poems are generally shorter in form than a sermon and the creative imagery engages the reader and lessens one's self-consciousness.

Many of the students were far from home and had no reason (and therefore were not allowed) to leave the seminary. So, early that fall I provided a reason, by inviting a few of the students to dinner at our house. Charley and Hank were from Ireland, which intrigued our daughters almost as much as their white habits. Each exuded polite behavior differently. Hank had a crew cut and was a man of few words. Charley's demeanor told me that he was convinced he'd say the wrong thing and do the wrong thing, both at the same time. His voice was unsure. The awkwardness was saved by the constant questions from my children about Ireland and the men's brogues. Pam repressed a giggle when Charley said, "I t'ink you would like Ireland." And, "I t'ink you girls are smart."

Despite its oddities, I liked the seminary. I loved soaking in liturgies in the warm-toned chapel. I admired the seminarians. In their awkward and devout ways, they reflected a desire to please God, not just the rector. Many of them were also very kind to me. I loved the seminary because God was not a topic to be avoided. God was a natural part of our conversations.

Regardless of Martha's earlier skepticism, I sensed no danger to myself in this beautiful place, sitting at the foot of a lovely New England mountain peak. In fact, I was amused when one of the seminarians tried to warn me about the hypocrisy and secrecy at the seminary. Matthew, the rector's secretary, took dictation from him every morning. He was told to kneel on the floor with his pen and book in hand, facing the rector sitting behind his large desk. Matthew had a sterling reputation for keeping all dictations secret. However, one morning I was meditating alone in the chapel and Matthew silently slid next to me.

In quick, halted whispers, he revealed what the rector had written about me to the provincial: "Mrs. Finn thinks the Church is a democracy. But have no fear, I intend to prove to her that it is a monarchy."

"But he only wrote to a provincial, not a bishop," I whispered back, trying to sort out the hierarchy embedded within the hierarchy of the Church. "Provincials have power, Mrs. Finn. The rector is worried because he claims you never had a day of Catholic education."

"He's right. I'm still Catholic."

Matthew seemed a bit shocked.

The preaching class was a challenge. The seminarians were smart, but the content of their presentations were lackluster. Their delivery was not much better. I could picture George and many others slowly dozing off in the pews during too many monotonous sermons. In desperation, I conceived a "Poetry Evening" at the seminary. My hope was that somehow the creative imagery of simple poems would eventually seep into the composition of their sermons.

Participation was voluntary, but the rush to the school's library to find the "best" poem resembled the rush of skiers down Mount Tom. The seminarians also needed an opportunity to speak in front of an audience. I decided to invite laypeople from the ecumenical council. The evening was a great success and my students began making progress. Gilbert took many photos; too many of them were of me.

In my own parish I was discovering how dismissive of creativity the Church could be. Katherine and Pamela were preparing for their

First Communion. My pregnancy confinement a few years earlier and then our move from Massachusetts to New Hampshire had postponed this sacred ritual for the girls, who were two years older than most of the children. When we went to the department store where Sister Mildred, who was in charge of preparing our children for this rite, had sent all the children to buy their Communion attire, but the outfits were a little "babyish" for the twins.

Buying two sets of dresses, veils, gloves, white prayer books, tights, and shoes would have cost more than $100. The girls urged me to make their clothes instead, "to save money," but surely fashion had something to do with it. "Mommy, please make our dresses. It will mean more to us," pleaded Pam. "And maybe even to God," Katherine slyly added.

The white dotted Swiss dresses were just what the girls wanted. They were appropriate and very pretty. But when we arrived at church, Sister Mildred was appalled. "Your girls will have to go at the end of the line. Dotted Swiss. What will it look like if they walk in with all the children who match?" The procession began with a contingent of girls dressed identically, then the boys. At the end, two tall girls, Pam and Katherine, each in their own unique, beautiful dress. The congregation smiled. If Sister Mildred was trying to keep me in line, it wasn't going to work.

When the parents mingled after the service, the pastor quietly took me aside. "Mrs. Finn, you may be good for the greater church someday, but you're not good for my parish. You're too creative."

I decided to keep my distance from the pastor, and the next time I went to confession, I choose to go to church a few towns over. But it seemed everyone had a different idea of how I could be useful. I entered the confessional. "Bless me, Father, for I have sinned. It's been two months since my last confession."

Through the screen I heard, "I saw you and I think I recognize your voice. You're the woman teaching at the seminary. Many of us are impressed by that." He paused.

I replied, "Do you want to hear my sins?"

Without answering me, he rushed on, "Well, there aren't many people that I can confide in and I think it's a sign from God that you are here. I'm having a devil of a time with celibacy, and I know how understanding you must be about this problem. I've fallen in love with someone." His voice, in whispers, was becoming less audible, but I heard him. "It's a terrible problem, because I still want to be a priest. She's taking that new pill, so we don't have to worry about…Well, you know what I mean. But she wants to get married…not go on like this…get married or break up. I'm in agony over it."

"Pardon me," I blurted. "I'm suddenly feeling dizzy. I've got to excuse myself." I quickly left the confessional.

He had picked a bad time and place for *his* confession. Several of the seminarians had sought my advice on their struggle with celibacy, but always in the privacy of my office. *Clearly, it's easier to speak with a* <u>*married*</u> *adult rather than with each other or with a superior.*

One day a second-year student named Liam made an appointment to see me in my office. He paced the floor in his disheveled white habit and ran his fingers through his hair. Finally he spoke. "Mother of Jesus, this place is still in the Dark Ages."

"Why's that Liam?

"Because the only thing the rector sees when he looks at us are virgins. He treats us like boys and expects the good lad behavior from us. Jaysus, we're men!"

"But with Vatican II, things are going to start opening up. Change will come," I offered.

"Not in the community."

I wondered what he meant exactly. "Do you want to be out of the community?" I asked apprehensively.

"No! I just want to be back in Dublin. I had dreams of the States. The movies I saw back home were marvelous, with exciting places and personal adventure. But we're stuck out here in the woods and can't even go to Keene."

I could only mirror his disappointment.

"The rector is such a pain in the arse." A grimace spread over Liam's broad face. "He refused to even discuss the stick-and-the-shower."

"The stick and..." I trailed off before Liam jumped in.

"In the shower...when we wash up. We have to keep our skivvies on and use a ruler with a sponge attached to it...to keep our privates safe from our hands." His head dropped. "It's so humiliating! Like, my body's some kind of enemy to who I am."

I was speechless. *Why did celibacy demand such extremes? It's as if the Holy Spirit is being kept by the rector under lock and key.*

2

A CHILD'S FAITH IN GOD

Driving From Keene To Boston, Summer 1965

The summer after my first year of teaching at Queen of Peace was devoted to driving to Boston and praying in hospitals. Pamela was born with cerebral palsy and required a leg brace and surgery. She was now eight, and falling frequently in chronic pain due to muscle weakness. Katherine also needed surgery for an internal kidney malfunction. I was fortunate that my parents, who were living in Easthampton, would help take care of our girls during our long trips to Boston.

Tommy and Blanche had mellowed and were getting along better in their older years. The cause for this miraculous case of domestic comfort sat in their living room—a Zenith television. Though each had their favorite programs, they both adored Fulton J. Sheen and Ed Sullivan. My father also liked Jackie Gleason. "The Irish Mafia," he called them.

Each of my three older daughters preferred Grandpa to Grandma, whom they felt was overbearing. As soon as I picked the girls up and we were out of earshot Katherine whined, "Grandma makes us say a decade of the rosary with her every day." Leslie reported, "She said the only way to Jesus is through Mary. And that we are getting mixed up because of all these changes from that Vatican II." Even Pam chimed in, "She doesn't think you should be at the seminary, because you don't belong there. What does she mean?"

My father stayed clear of church talk; instead he would take Leslie, Katherine, and Pam for quiet walks into town. Then he would treat the girls to hot fudge sundaes and a chat. Tierney was only three and stayed back with Grandma, whom she loved. My mother always had new dresses, hair bows, and a quart glass bottle filled with colorful buttons waiting for Tierney.

The only tension that spoiled our visits emerged from the Vietnam War, which my father vigorously supported and George just as vigorously opposed. As a testimony to both, their spats went sideways instead of head-on and usually took place only when war stories ran on the television news. Fortunately, family politics did not spill over into in the dining room, mainly because my father was absent from the table. When I was a child, he had frequent alcohol-induced outbursts and my mother had banned him from eating with the rest of the family. Although he stopped drinking when I was eighteen, out of habit he still ate, alone, in the kitchen.

At the end of the summer, our prayers were answered. Our twin's surgeries were a success. Pamela's surgeon, Dr. Banks, became her favorite person. In the hospital, the night before her operation, I tried to help Pam fall asleep. She was looking small but spunky, wrapped in white hospital sheets; she insisted we play Animal, Vegetable, Mineral over and over. Finally her eyelids were drooping behind her thick glasses.

"This is the last game, Pam."

"Okay, Mommy. It's not an animal or a vegetable or a mineral, but in a way it's all of those things."

"Is it the sky?"

"Nope."

"Is it the soil where animals live, vegetables grow, and you can find minerals?"

"Nope. You silly, it's God." She smiled and took my breath away. "And God is in Dr. Banks' hands."

"You're right. God is everywhere, especially in your heart."

She nodded off to sleep. I removed her glasses and kissed her brow. That was the start of my twenty-four hour prayer marathon. Pam was right about God and Dr. Banks. She recuperated after the successful operation at the Boston Children's Hospital, with George and I taking turns at her bedside.

3

TEACHING PREACHING

Keene, New Hampshire, 1965

On the first day of my second fall semester at Queen of Peace, Fr. Gilbert called me into his office. I sensed a difference in him. He was more formal, more old school "priestly." Sitting behind his desk, he pontificated about "changes" that needed to be made. To me they sounded like regressions. "The provincial thinks things went too far last year. We became lapse in how the seminary is run. Holy books on doctrine will be read aloud during lunch and artwork will be removed from the walls. Because he is my superior, I must agree with him."

Last year went too far? In my mind, the cultural shift had not gotten as far as the corner. How could grown men worry about such trivial things?

"The provincial wants me to make clear your parameters," Gilbert intoned.

"Parameters?"

"Yes. You are to be restricted to your office, your classroom, and the chapel, except for the refectory. No chatting in the halls or outside with the seminarians. No wandering the corridors—"

"Gilbert, I never wandered the corridors." The intensity of his eyes and the jut of his chin bothered me, as much as what he was saying.

"You tried to join us in the priest's lounge."

"Once! It is also the faculty lounge." My slow burn intensified with each word.

As if I hadn't interrupted him, Gilbert marched on. "You are to use only one bathroom—the guest bathroom on the first floor. That will be yours. The rest of the house is off-limits."

As my head pounded, Gilbert stood up. "Let me show you your new office—it's on this floor." He smiled. "It's bigger than the space you had last year and it's near my office."

We walked a few feet down the dark corridor. He opened the door.

"No. It's out of the question. There's a bed in here." I pointed to the faded yellow chenille bedspread. *Does he not see that this encourages the seminarians to get closer to me? Does he not notice that temptation is being mandated from above?* "I cannot meet one-on-one with seminarians in a room with a bed in it. Don't you see how this would be inappropriate?"

"Hmm. I will look for another office."

On my next day at work, a cubbyhole next to the bedroom was offered to me. It was small, dark, and musty. Previously it had been a storeroom for paraphernalia like monstrances, hair shirts, and kneelers.

Despite the new parameters placed on me because of my gender, I'd be damned rather than be cautious.

"Show Me," a song from the popular film *My Fair Lady,* became the theme of my homiletics course. I wanted the students to show and reveal the depth of the gospels, rather than simply feed the parishioners a theological analysis of the gospel readings. As the men filed into the classroom, they heard the song and their enthusiasm stepped up a beat.

I explained to them that one of the things Vatican II had revealed was that giving sermons based solely on doctrinal instruction was not actually ministering to God's people. In reviewing portions of the *Sacrosanctum Concilium*, also known as the Constitution of the Sacred Liturgy, we studied how the term "sermon" was frequently being replaced by the term "homily" and that a homily should draw its content mainly from scriptural reflection. It is not the place for providing religious instruction or Christian doctrine.

The Second Vatican Council also had stressed the significance of preaching by the bishops and priests as workers for the kingdom of God. The seminarians were enthralled with these concepts. They were particularly attentive when I referred to the document's emphasis that the homilies apply "concrete circumstances of life and the particular needs of hearers."

Referring to the upcoming Sunday gospel reading, Luke's parable of the good Samaritan, I read them two different examples of homilies. The first was an example of the more traditional style: the connection to the second commandment; the revelation that universal salvation is available for all, regardless of a person's status; and the growing animosity between Jesus and the religious leaders.

For my second sermon, I shared a story about my quest with George to help Pamela with her cerebral palsy.

"We had visited every doctor in our area and gone on several long trips to meet with specialists in Boston. Each doctor was dismissive, saying that Pam's physical disabilities were so severe that she should be placed in an institution for the disabled. Finally, we met Dr. Banks at Boston Children's Hospital. This "good Samaritan" took the time to do a thorough diagnosis, independent research, and surgery. Because of him, my daughter was making great strides and the word 'institution' would never be heard in our family again."

One of the seminarians quietly asked, "But we're so isolated in the seminary. We're never allowed to go near the people in the pews, so how are we supposed to know the circumstances of their lives and their needs?"

"You've got a point. But after you're ordained, you will get to know your parishioners," I encouraged.

"Maybe," he grumbled. "But it feels like it will be forever until that happens."

"Well, for now you have your own life. And I'm going to suggest that you dig down into your own experience and see where it connects to a gospel scene. Wisdom suggests that we give a personal response before we create a public response. Let's not skim the top. Read through an entire passage."

The silence in the classroom was audible. "Your assignment for the next class is to take a gospel passage and reflect on when you have felt like someone in a story that Jesus told. Or in a healing performed by Jesus."

"You expect us to spill our guts to everyone else in the class?" demanded one of the older students.

What was their resistance? I was only asking that they make a connection between life and a parable.

"Just find a link in your life and share it, " I suggested.

"What if we don't want to?" one student boldly shouted. "Are you going to report us to Rector Brendan?"

"No. Why would I? Just give it a try."

When the students walked into class the next day, they found the chairs moved into a circle. I hoped to facilitate a more communal environment. The seminarians were looking awkwardly at the floor. Then one of the younger men broke the silence with a short, funny analogy. "Whenever I hear the Gospel of Mark 3:3, Jesus healing on the Sabbath, I think of the man with the withered arm. And I think of what is withering on me. And I guarantee you it's not my arm or my heart."

The students' laughter broke the ice and others began to share their homilies. Patrick, one of the older men, had also chosen the story of the good Samaritan.

"When I was in the novitiate in Ireland, the novice master had us dig a long ditch at the back of the property to be used for a new pipe. It was winter and we weren't given gloves. Fasting was instituted. We dug for over a week. The next week, the novice master told us the pipe was going elsewhere and so we dug another long ditch, through the rain and mud. During dinner on the final day of digging, the novice master announced that there was no pipe to lay in the ditches. There had never been any intention of laying a pipe. 'You men need toughening up. There is no rest for the wicked. Suffering brings you closer to Jesus.'"

I quietly nudged Patrick to complete his reflection. "Who were you in the parable?" I asked.

He slowly and cautiously replied, "The victim. The victim in the ditch."

Students began to meet one-on-one with me in my shabby office. They wanted to share with someone who was not part of their hierarchy. When Charley came in one day, I learned why. Suspicion was rife at the seminary.

"I'm really upset with the stuff going on here. I vowed not to tell anybody, but I need to speak with someone. You won't tell any of the fathers, will you?"

I reassured Charley. "You know I won't. And I certainly won't tell the rector."

"Well, each seminarian is assigned two priests; a spiritual director and a confessor. We meet separately each week."

"Yes, Charley. I think that is a good thing. You are not only practicing the work you will be doing outside the seminary, but you are also deepening your own faith."

"Yes, but, Fr. Brendan has been asking some of us what is being said in our conferences."

"Charley, I don't understand."

"Brendan is snooping! It doesn't seem right to me. He's spying."

"But, you are not allowed to repeat what is said during confession."

"No, no. *Technically*, the priest is under the seal of the confession, but the *penitent* can reveal what is said. Brendan is looking for informers."

"Has anyone asked what his motivation is?"

"He proclaims 'community life,'" Charley groaned. "It's for 'the good of the order.' But he is simply checking up on us. Making sure no one is defiling himself or thinking of leaving the priesthood. Please, Virginia, don't share this with anyone. The other seminarians are counting on me to do something. I have to think about how to handle it without causing trouble."

" Of course I won't. I respect the seal of confidentiality."

Soon I began having misgivings about my Church. Suspicion is contagious. It didn't dawn on me that even I was becoming suspicious. I began wearing a hat in the chapel despite the dispensation on women and hats from the Second Vatican Council. I stayed clear of the very rebels, like Charley, who might cause a stir. However, during Lent I was called into Gilbert's office and told that the "powers that be" wanted me to leave.

"They want me to leave—"

"Yes." He looked down at his shoes. "I was told to say that you personalize your classes too much. It's upsetting to the order of the place."

"I am teaching the way I was trained to teach when I got a Master's in Education. Professional teachers let their students ask questions. They listen and evaluate their students' presentations, just like I do. And now my students are beginning to give the best homilies I have ever heard."

"The provincial and the rector are quite insistent."

"Well, I'm not interested in resigning. I owe it to the students to stay until the ordination, at the end of the year. Tell the provincial he will have to fire me."

"But how can they fire you without gossip? You might tell people, people in Keene. The provincial and the rector want to avoid—"

"A scandal."

"Yes. A scandal in town. And they don't know how to fire anyone." He looked away again, this time to a window. "You're the only 'employee' we've ever had."

"Tell the 'powers that be' that I refuse to quit. They will have to fire me, at the end of the year. I am staying until then, and I expect to receive my paycheck."

I stayed on until the ordination and was paid every week.

The ordination was a special day. The seminarians' families from "outside the community" came with pride in their hearts, with flowers in hands, and wearing their finery. My family and I came too. George in his best suit. The twins in their beautiful First Communion dresses. Leslie in a new party dress, and Tierney, tugging on a bonnet I'd tied under her chin. Everyone sat patiently in the pew.

As the service began and the music started, sadness fell over me. The blessing of superb singing comes with a seminary, and I knew I'd miss these voices. Then the doors opened in the back of the church, and the white-habited procession came down the center of the aisle. I was swept up in the celebration. Each ordinate carried a folded vestment of priesthood over his left arm and a lighted candle in his right hand.

The ceremony began with formal presentations to "the most reverend father and ruler in Christ, His Excellency . . . by the grace of God and of the Apostolic See, bishop of the Diocese of Manchester." Then the name of each ordinate was read aloud, the seminarian stepped forward, and replied, "Present." My heart rejoiced for each of my former students. The girls quietly clapped for Charley and for Hank.

Next, an assistant read an interdict, a last warning that if anyone received the sacrament under false pretenses, he would incur the penalty of excommunication. *Hmmm.* The ceremony proceeded with various prayers and rituals. When the Litany of the Saints began, parents, siblings, aunts, and uncles leaned over each other to view the candidates, lying prostrate on the floor. Leslie quietly began asking me questions. "I'll explain later," I whispered to my girls.

The service continued with the laying of the hands, vesting of the new priests, and Mass. The beauty of the ritual filled me with great joy.

Before I knew it, the ceremony ended and everyone proceeded outside. My girls, who had been especially patient during the two hours, were thrilled to run around in the fresh air. I was humbled to kneel in front of Patrick for the privilege of his First Blessing. Although I was bitter at being fired from Queen of Peace, I enjoyed a bountiful repast in the rectory with my students and some of my colleagues, and that provided me solace.

4

SOCIAL JUSTICE IN AN URBAN MAZE

Springfield, Massachusetts, 1968

George took another job and we moved back to Massachusetts.
In 1968, Springfield ranked as the 18th most dangerous city in the nation.

Change is a constant in my family. During my last months at the seminary, George had begun expressing disillusionment with his job. I suggested he look beyond the manufacturing sector, hoping that a new career would help him stay with one job and improve his mood. George began actively searching for other options and his disposition did improve. Before long, a new position became available, in a new field, in a new town. And so, we moved back to Massachusetts.

My first morning living in Springfield, I was awakened by a ringing sound that I thought was in my dream. But I reached for the receiver by the bed anyway. "Hullo." I heard my own grogginess.

"Mrs. Finn? You alright?"

I immediately recognized the voice of my new boss on the other end.

"I'm tired. We just moved yesterday."

"Okay, that explains why you weren't here on time to start your consulting position."

"I'm so sorry!" I sprang up in bed, startled by the realization of my own lapse.

As an initiation into urban life, and a way to do some social justice work, I had accepted a part-time teaching position in a Head Start program a month before our move to Springfield.

I was absent the very first day. "Shall I come now?" I suggested.

"Hey, come next week at the same time. Head Start's not going anywhere. You take it easy now."

The happy contrast between my new employer's attitude and that of the officials at the seminary lifted me off the bed. Our expansive new home, with two staircases, three floors, and three bathrooms, was probably built for a robber baron. But the ostentatious house was a perk that came with George's new position as the business manager at The MacDuffie School, an elite private high school for girls.

I made my way downstairs to eat some breakfast, but found chaos everywhere. A few minutes later, George arrived home.

"Honey? Honey?"

What a relief. He's home to help.

"I'm in here. The living room."

"Oh, there you are. I thought I'd stop in to see how it's going?"

"Well, why is all the furniture down here? Did the movers forget to put it away?" I asked.

George explained that workers from the school would come by later to move the furniture. He rummaged around, found my suitcase, and handed it to me. "Here, you can just dress in the downstairs bath. Then you can take the car and shop for the groceries. And while you're out, you can look for some curtains for the house."

Curtains? Just three years ago I made curtains for our house in New Hampshire!

" And tonight. Don't bother cooking dinner."

"I didn't intend to." *Where was another suitcase I could throw at him?*

"Honey, I love my new job. Try to be happy. Will you do that for me?" His dark eyes were begging as well as his voice.

On the following Sunday, we explored our neighborhood and attended Mass at the nearby cathedral. We decided to try it, as we had no idea where our local parish might be.

George muttered as I dipped my hand in the holy water fount, "I'm not sure about this."

"It will be okay. The bishop from this diocese went to Rome for Vatican II," I whispered to George, as we sat in a pew partway down the nave.

He whispered back, "Yep, he must have. The altar's turned around and Mass is in English."

But the old-fashioned language from the *Confraternity of Christian Doctrine* was the English used in the homily. The priest urged the parishioners in the pews to convert our Protestant, and even Jewish, neighbors. "Be fishers of men!" the priest boomed. *"Fishers of men." That's an outdated term.*

"You have the faith, the treasure that they lack. So go be fishers of men."

My breakfast rose into my throat. *God, where is the ecumenism here? Where's working together with other faiths? We are reverting back to converting.*

That week I met Mattie, a Baptist who had more faith in Jesus Christ than most laypeople or clergy that I have known, and she became my savior on many levels. A faculty member had recommended

Mattie, 'a dependable housekeeper.' I was uncomfortable with the idea of someone working for me as a cleaning lady, but am forever grateful that Mattie was brought into my life. She became a babysitter, a confidante, and a role model. Tall, but fully rounded in a way that made her motherly, she kept her hair tight to her head with a net, always wore a housedress, and was the best gift Springfield gave me.

The first day she came to clean, we were working together in my refrigerator. I handed her a package of cheese and asked her to throw it in the garbage.

"Why?" she asked. Her head cocked to the side.

"It's moldy," I replied.

"You just scrape off that mold, Mrs. Finn. It'll be fine."

I lifted my shoulders in surprise. "Well, we don't usually do that."

"Well, I do. You mind if I take it home?" Then she pointed to the bottom shelf. "If it isn't too much trouble, Mrs. Finn, if you ever think of throwing out anything else from the fridge, would you put it there and let me get a look first?"

Mattie didn't live alone. She had a sister, Willie Mae, and another who was disabled. Five children also lived with them though I wasn't sure who belonged to whom. I did know what a blessing and saving grace Mattie was for me, and how she took to Tierney and how Tierney took to her.

When I went to work, Mattie would take care of Tierney. Her son Clarence would come over and the kids played together, exploring the large house.

One night Tierney sat upright at the dining room table, hands folded, her curls rolled every which way. "Tonight we must pray for Brother Benjamin. C'mon everybody, fold your hands."

"I'm not going to pray for someone I've never heard of," Katherine said, putting her hands in her lap. "Who is he?"

"Brother Benjamin is part of Mattie's church. He's very sick. We visited him this afternoon." Tierney forgot about praying and dove into her bowl of chili.

"Where does he live?" George asked. "How did you get there?"

"By bus. Mattie held my hand the whole way, so don't worry, Daddy." She wiped her mouth. "It was pretty far—very far, but in the city. Brother Benjamin is so poor. One of his windows is broken. And he has newspapers instead of a rug on the floor." Tierney put down her spoon and closed her eyes. "Now let's pray for Brother Benjamin. I promised Mattie that we would." We all rested our spoons and did her bidding.

Unfortunately, because Pamela had to wear a metal brace on one of her legs, which extended from her toe up to her knee, she became an easy target for both her peers and strangers. She and Katherine went to Ursuline Academy, a fifteen-minute walk from the house. Leslie was in junior high at George's school. Soon after moving in, a neighbor knocked on the door to alert me to what was happening outside.

Three teenage girls had chased Pam and Katherine home from school. Peering out the front window, I saw the twins pinned to the ground with Pam being punched. I raced out the front door, screaming at the top of my lungs. The teenagers looked at me and fled. With my arms around both girls, we went into the house. Their knees were bloody, their uniforms torn, and their spirits shaken.

When George came home that night, he was concerned but was reluctant to leave his job at the school. *Well, of course. The school has a nice campus. A safe, idyllic campus.*

"Did you also know that the place next to Mattie's was broken into just last week?" I heard my voice escalating.

He put his arms around me. "I will keep you safe. I love my work here and I love you. Nothing will happen."

When he said that, I felt guilty. I was glad he'd found work he loved but I wished he loved it somewhere else. In the middle of the night I often woke up thinking my father, drunk, was trying to get in the house. Then I wondered if it was a break-in. The summer we moved in, there had been five murders in our vicinity.

Chris, a German Shepherd, joined our family the next weekend to help the girls and I feel safer. Chris instantly became attached to Tierney as if he were her very own Secret Service agent. Snarling and barking, he was ready to lunge at any children who came to play out our house. But if any adult came to the door, he wagged his tail and smiled. Tierney now felt more at ease, but the other girls and I still were restless.

One afternoon I was in the sunroom with papers spread over the table preparing for my next class at Head Start. I heard the doorbell ring. Chris happily followed me to the front door. Hesitantly, I opened the door and it was Gilbert, from the seminary.

"Come in." I gave a warning to the dog. "Chris, this is Fr. Gilbert. He's very nice, so please behave." Just to be safe, I took Chris into the sunroom and closed the door.

Gilbert was sitting on the sofa when I entered the living room. "Where are your girls?"

"The older ones are in school and my babysitter to our youngest to the library, so I can prepare for my class. I'm teaching at a Head Start program and at Springfield College. Come in the living room."

"Just as well they're out. I am in Springfield for a conference, which is convenient, because I wanted to tell you something." He paused. Shifted on the sofa. Rubbed his mouth with his hand. "I'm leaving."

"The conference? Is it boring?"

"No, no," he chuckled. "The religious order."

"That's a surprise. You'd rather be a parish priest?"

"Ginny, I'm leaving the priesthood."

I should offer him something to drink. "Are you thirsty?"

"Yes, but don't bother getting me anything. I really can't stay. I'm thirsty for marriage. There's a Sister; she's leaving her order as well. We'll be getting married. Our wedding is next fall. I hope you and your husband will be there."

"That's very kind of you to invite us. But I can't believe you're leaving the priesthood."

"Well, that's not all. You were crucial in this decision. And I wanted to . . . well, get it off my chest, I guess."

"Get what off your chest?" *Why on earth am I crucial?*

"Well, I didn't think that you would ever leave George, but if you did, I hoped it would be for a priest." He squirmed on the sofa.

No, no. What is he saying?

"But, Ginny, I want to share that when you were meeting last year with seminarians in the afternoon, I was in the next room, with a *Playboy* magazine. I fantasized about you and me, and pleasured myself."

No, no. God, please no.

"In the room next to my office? How often?"

"Every single time that I could be there." He looked almost proud of the feat. "What can I say?"

That you're sorry. But he didn't say that.

"I know you're upset by my leaving the priesthood. But, I want you to meet Margaret, my bride-to-be. You'll like her."

Inside I was shaking, but I kept my arms, legs, and face rigid. "You have to get back to that conference. . . " I didn't want to look at him, so I spoke to the window.

He stood. "Sure. Look for the wedding invitation in the mail if we don't get together before then."

I didn't respond. He let himself out. When I heard the motor start, I raced up the stairs, thrust on the faucets in the bath, shed my clothes, and, once in the tub, I was fierce about lathering my arms, legs, chest, all of me. *I have to get it off, his thoughts, those images, him.*

I saturated water and soap all over. "Off, off, off!" I shouted until my skin looked red and felt raw.

Out of the tub, I scrubbed my body with two towels. When I caught a glimpse of my face in the mirror, I told myself that I hated it. I put on pajamas, climbed into bed, and covered all of me, including my head, with the sheet and blanket.

He never asked me to forgive him…Why should he? You were the thing that tempted him.

Mattie returned to the house and let the dog out. He'd been barking for half an hour out in the sunroom. She found me in bed. I asked her to stay at the house until the older girls were back from school. They returned and I asked them to watch Tierney. George got back from work. I told him to take the kids out for supper and tend to them until bedtime.

Bedtime came and went that day and the next. Mattie watched Tierney. When it was almost time to leave for work, I got up, dressed, and went off to teach. I could lose my mind, but the one thing I could not lose was my job.

The next week, I clamped myself onto the routine of the house. By rote I went about the business of mother, wife, cook, laundress, and listener. Underneath accomplishing tasks and reporting to work, I wandered through a dark and primitive undergrowth of terror and guilt. *God doesn't want me at the seminary, or anywhere near a church, to tempt seminarians and priests with my body. God didn't want me period.*

Mirrors forgot what I looked like because they never saw my face. At the beauty shop, I asked the hairdresser to turn the chair toward the window without telling her I wanted to avoid the mirror. She followed my request for bangs and a short bob without knowing they enabled me to brush my hair with no help from a mirror.

George took the girls to church on Sundays. I went only if it was at the small Franciscan chapel. There was the problem of Communion. Receiving was no longer my right. But not receiving Communion led to too many questions from my daughters. I didn't tell George about Gilbert because I was afraid he'd go and beat him up. Each day I read something from Scripture. The psalms, at times, consoled me.

For my birthday in March, George had planned a surprise. Arrangements had been made with my mother to have the children for the weekend while he and I spent two nights at the Hotel Northampton, where our wedding reception had been held.

We had recently learned that Pope Paul VI, rejecting the recommendations of his lay advisers, issued *Humanae Vitae*, and insisted that using birth control was still a sin. George was furious. So in this beautiful, quiet, romantic setting we celebrated our rebellion against Pope Paul VI's recent ban on birth control. I lay in bed with George's arms circling me. His strength eased my fears, and I was able to forget the shock from Gilbert.

It had been good to get away from Springfield for a few days with George. But in April, Martin Luther King, Jr. was assassinated. It stunned and saddened us. That it rocked the city was no surprise. That night Mattie called us.

"Don't none of you go to Winchester Square tonight. Some of our own boys are up to no good up. You need to stay home."

"Okay, Mattie, I won't." Winchester Square was the main shopping district in Springfield. "But, it's happening all over. They're just reacting." I reassured her.

"That don't help poor Rev. King's wife. Please tell Mr. Finn. Even he should stay away from Winchester Square."

Civil rights did not seem to be Mattie's cause. Behave yourself was the one lesson she insisted on for the children in her house.

When Robert F. Kennedy was murdered only two months after, there were riots and two more murders in a nearby neighborhood. All I wanted was to get away from crime, fear, loneliness. I wanted flight. None of our old friends would visit us. They felt it was too dangerous.

The sense of community that we longed for was not present in the schools, neighborhoods, or church. Although Mattie's neighborhood was very unsafe, at least she had community. On Sunday, she invited our family to her church and I savored its vibrant spirit and gospel music. After, the Sunday dinner in her home was jammed with relatives and friends. I saw that Mattie had community with an organic vitality; something I envied, something that made the community in the religious order I'd known seem a sham. In Mattie's community, they needed one another to survive. Perhaps, I told myself, that is the key to communal life.

The last straw for me in Springfield came with a phone call one evening, as I was beginning to settle Tierney into bed. It was the mother of Tierney's Puerto Rican friend, Alicia. She wanted to know if her daughter was with us. She had gone out to play before supper and still hadn't returned.

When George told Alicia's mom that her daughter wasn't at our house, she asked if he'd join a group scouring the neighborhood, and he did. The hours crawled by. I prayed. Tried to watch television. Finally, around 11:30, I heard Chris bark. I went to the door. George was home, and Alicia was alive. They had found her in a vacant house, on the porch. She was there with a homeless drug addict.

"Did he . . . was she hurt?"

"They won't know for sure until the morning. They're bringing her to the hospital. Alicia was sobbing. Scared out of her wits."

He put his head into his hands. "All I thought of was the girls. I won't be able to sleep."

"Let me get you a drink."

"Tomorrow, or sometime this week, I'll start a search for another job. We can't take any more chances with the kids living in the city. If they aren't penned up in school, they have to be penned up at home. We aren't doing a damn bit of good for anybody here anyway. The problems of this city are beyond us. And you're certainly not thriving."

5

THE BERKSHIRES AND THE
VINEYARD COMMUNITY

Lenox, Massachusetts, Early 1970s

The Vineyard Community was formed by Jesuit priests, myself, and other laypeople. It was an expansion of the parish at a private Catholic boys high school. The Vineyard blended the arts, participation of the parishioners, spirituality, and community between the priests and laypeople.

Safe at last! Berkshire County was nirvana to me. My heart ached for anybody in this nation of ours who had to live with the violence that seemed to be engulfing many urban areas, Springfield among them.

Berkshire County, nestled in the far western region of Massachusetts, had quaint cities and towns, each with its own history and beauty. Our cozy home was in Lenox at the foot of a Berkshire Hill.

The first week we lived in Lenox, we noticed that our neighbors did not bother locking their doors. *Can trust be taken for granted here?*

Our backyard had two red barns, an old stone well by a gazebo, and a trail that led up to a mountainous park. On our first visit there in the late spring, a carpet of forget-me-nots welcomed us. I sensed my body falling into an embrace of this beautiful county, the Berkshires, where my father had found hope as a boy. I was home again.

After our young neighbor Alicia was found in that empty house in Springfield, George wasted no time planning our next move. He soon secured a new job. He was torn about leaving The McDuffie School. He enjoyed his work and the students loved his warmth and humor. Just before he left the school, George had set up a small recreation room, with vending machines, and tables and chairs. They called it Finn's Bin, a name that remains today, though the school was sold and relocated. Ursuline Academy, Pamela and Katherine's school, was also relocated to a safer area.

His new position in Lenox was as the business manager of Windsor Mountain School, a private high school that was only a fifteen-minute walk from our house. Upon being hired, George was told that the school had at its core "progressive" education principles. The school was run by Europeans with strong political views. There was no dress code, none of the student publications were reviewed by the staff, and the student government determined and implemented *all* nonacademic guidelines. The school's philosophy was that by giving students extensive freedoms, they would become self-directed individuals, citizens of the world. Windsor Mountain was on the cutting edge of the 1970s.

It worried me for the girl's sake that moving again meant shifts in schooling and friends. But there were many benefits, including guest passes to Tanglewood through George's school. Tanglewood is the home of the Boston Symphony Orchestra in the summer. During their performances, I would lay on a blanket gazing up at the stars, feeling the transcendent pull to the heavens. The girls were granted permission to attend one rock concert for every one classical concert they attended. Harmony in the family reigned.

One evening, our three older daughters took advantage of the free passes. They came home excited and energized.

"The concert was so cool!"

"Who was it?" I asked.

"The Who," Katherine responded.

"That's what I asked—who?" I said.

"*THE* Who. It's a rock band," Leslie clarified.

There were two churches in our town, and George and I visited the Catholic parish. In the process, we read in the local paper that a beautiful, modern chapel had just been built at Cranwell Preparatory School, a Catholic school for boys in Lenox. Each Sunday, they held liturgy there for the students. George and I decided to try it.

One morning, at the coffee hour after church, George spoke with one of the teachers, Fr. Ed Hallen. He mentioned a new type of Mass, a "Home Mass." I had never heard of a Home Mass, but George was proud to be ahead of the times and invited Fr. Ed to our house to lead a Home Mass.

"But will it count?" I asked George.

"Of course! Vatican II has happened. Why are you still back where your mother is? Sweetie, loosen up. Have some faith in God."

And the next Sunday, I did. Expecting a priest dressed like a hippy in jeans and a batik shirt, I sighed with relief when Fr. Ed filled our doorway with his clerical black clothes, neatly groomed, short brown hair, and kind eyes. His soft voice was accepting of us, and our small living room was soon crowded with members of Ed's Home Mass group.

Ten kids were on the floor, adult guests on our red plaid sofa and straight-backed chairs, while Ed sat in our best chair with a small table in front of him. On the table were pita bread and wine. Ed wore a simple stole, and after the readings, he started the homily and then invited us to add our reflections.

At first there was an awkward silence. *Please, someone say something.* Slowly, the adults and some of the older children shared their responses. Some were questions for Ed to further explain the context of the reading within the Jewish tenets of Jesus' time. Others shared how they felt the gospel was present in their own lives today.

When Ed moved into the eucharistic prayer, I felt no reservations, only a blessing that filled the room like the sun. We passed around the consecrated bread. Soon our family was a regular part of the Home Mass group, which alternated between homes in towns spread throughout Berkshire County. The times that Ed was unavailable, we went to Cranwell for liturgy.

In the Berkshires we were meeting a variegated garden of new friends, which was a refreshing experience. Through Sarah, a neighbor, I joined the League of Women Voters. She explained that the league was trying to expand the group and find more women of diversity. *I don't think I've seen more than five black people in Lenox?* But Sarah was referring to religious diversity.

At the first meeting I attended, I was one of four Catholic women and two Jewish women, where previously there had only been Protestant women. As the league coordinator, Sarah introduced the first topic: the movement to abolish the Massachusetts blue laws. *That's fine. I'm okay with grocery shopping after church on Sunday.*

The next discussion turned to the laws that forbade birth control and abortion. One of the Catholic women, Paula, immediately spoke up. She agreed that laws against contraception were outdated, but was shocked that anyone would even consider terminating a pregnancy.

"I can't have any children," she sobbed. "How can you end a pregnancy . . . Aren't they babies? No, no, no."

"We're only discussing the right to terminate in the early weeks of a pregnancy," Sarah clarified.

One of the other Catholic women, Nancy, was also very uncomfortable. "I don't think I should be here . . . I don't want anyone to know that I was here."

Those two never returned to the group, which left Joyce and I as the token Catholics. Molly hosted the next meeting. She was a petite woman with dark, curly hair, who met me at the door carrying her baby son.

Molly led me into a living room, which was twice the size of mine. Sarah asked if anyone wanted to share personal stories pertaining to pregnancy, an important topic for each woman.

"Molly, are you willing to open—"

"Yes."

Molly moved over to a wing chair by the fireplace, patting the baby. "We had three other children. When they started school, I loved being at home with the kids, so we embarked on another pregnancy. But soon after I had troubles. I was diagnosed with cervical cancer."

Molly paused for a sip of the iced drink Sarah had handed her. "The treatment for the cancer ensured a bad effect on the baby I was carrying. It wasn't an easy decision."

Listening, I held my breath. I was actually hearing a woman say she'd had an abortion, and in the presence of others. Molly lowered her eyes, placed her drink on the flagstone hearth. "But we went ahead and had the abortion, the cancer treatment, and three years later, I was expecting again. Here is the beautiful fruit of that pregnancy." Her eyes teared. "God is good."

My eyes slightly watered.

Dressed more formally than the rest of us, one woman had draped a silk scarf near her neck and tied her gray hair into a French twist. "Why do you New Englanders share everything, top to bottom, out on a living room floor? It's something I'll never understand. Don't you believe in privacy?" She adjusted her scarf. "In the South you have a little problem, you take yourself off to the family doctor who takes care of it. Nobody the wiser. Not even your hubby."

"Not everyone in Massachusetts has a regular doctor. And not all doctors will do this." Sarah was composed. "Changing the law will protect doctors as well as women."

"And let them prescribe the pill legally," another woman added.

"But birth control pills aren't needed!" Joyce spoke up forcefully. She launched into a lecture on why the rhythm method showed that no woman needed contraceptives. She gave a detailed description on how to track when you ovulate—monitor your body temperature every day, check your cervical secretions, record the length of each period on a chart. "That is the birth control that God created."

"My husband and I tried that method," I blurted out. Another Catholic story needed to be told.

My mind slipped back in time. "I had three children and then I had five miscarriages. During my last miscarriage, I was cramping, in terrible pain, and bleeding. I called my husband George and begged him to hurry home. By the time George arrived, the fetus had slipped out when I was in the bathroom.

"I called the doctor who told me to simply flush the toilet. I couldn't bear to, so I asked George to do it. He said it was 'something he shouldn't have to do.' I called our priest and asked him if we could have a burial. The priest told me that 'burials are only for full-term stillborns.'

"Finally I did as the doctor instructed. Then I collapsed in bed, still bleeding."

I stopped speaking and bowed my head to avoid looking any of the women in the eye. The woman next to me put her arm around me. Then Sarah asked if I had ever been pregnant again.

With my head still down, I murmured, "Yes." Then I lifted my head. "We started using birth control so my body could recover. When I got pregnant, the blessing was Tierney. She's now five. Happy, healthy. She loves to dance!" I smiled, then gazed at the women around me. Never before had I found the courage to tell that story.

"What did you learn from it?" Molly asked.

"Not to trust men when it comes to my body. Only women bear children." Though I didn't slump in my chair, within myself I was drained.

How I navigated the car back to Lenox that night is a wonder. Never had I experienced such open sharing. Surely never at a gathering of Catholic women, or among Catholic couples, or with priests, who believed they had all the answers about what to do with our female bodies.

The following day, the saying 'Mother knows best' echoed in my head. Fathers in the Church don't realize how many opportunities God gives women and men to procreate. From adolescence through menopause a woman has at least four hundred chances to become pregnant. I felt energized by a discussion with a secular organization, which I had viewed as a group of uptight ladies. My mind had changed. Still, I was disappointed that within Catholic circles we hesitated to speak our truths.

6

THE BODY AND THE WHEEL

Lenox, Massachusetts, 1972

The Body and the Wheel is a play by William Gibson and was presented at Cranwell Preparatory.

"Jesus, one foot each will be enough," instructed our director.

The washing of the feet doesn't just happen. Disciples stand, stretch, then sit again on steps leading to the altar; this time with only one foot in readiness for washing. Jesus approaches and kneels at Peter's feet. Children from wandering tribes are scattered on a narrow ledge beneath stained-glass windows, rose and blue in abstract design. Beneath an altar, in a small chapel honoring Mary, the Crowd waits in a tight cluster, humming the *Agnus Dei*. Backstage, the High Priests are practicing their lines, Lazarus is reading, and Martha is knitting. At the foot of the center aisle, the director contemplates his stage directions.

The people of the Vineyard Community were becoming a 'gospel people' during the rehearsal process of *The Body and the Wheel*. Bill Gibson based the play on the life of Jesus as told in the New Testament. Every line of dialogue is directly from the gospels. The actors were priests and students from Cranwell, and adults and children who attended mass there. We rehearsed a few nights a week in the church, under Bill's direction.

George and I had met Bill at a theological seminar held at Cranwell. Bill was gentle and unassuming, despite having received a Tony Award and an Oscar nomination for his play and movie, *The Miracle Worker.* He had a Catholic mother, a Protestant father, and was married to a psychoanalyst.

Bill often met with me to talk about his spiritual life. He also liked to go on expeditions, like hiking alone to the base of the Grand Canyon. One day George received a postcard from Mexico with two simple lines: "I've written a play. Be back soon. Bill."

The Body and the Wheel is a beautiful and transformative work. After a prologue from John the Baptist, the script starts with Jesus' forty days of temptation in the desert, and culminates with the crucifixion and resurrection. It's not a play with a lot of props or scenery; Bill infused the production with lighting, music, and liturgical dance. It was clear that Bill wrote it with the Cranwell Chapel in mind.

The chapel was designed to reveal space in a structure of light and color on a grand scale. That it was. It was circular and rested on top of a Berkshire Hill. The walls, graced by modern stained glass windows, soared high, as if stretching to the heavens. The simple wooden pews were arranged around the stone altar, which was approached from a tier of round broad steps. During the production of *The Body and the Wheel,* Bill used many of the hidden spaces as entrances and exits for the actors. The to-and-fro movement created a profoundly transformed relationship to a holy space.

Each Lent, the Vineyard Community's liturgical arts committee, which was led by local artists John and Primm ffrench, hung a majestic banner high above the altar. It remained there for the forty days until Holy Saturday. That year the banner spelled out the word COMMITMENT.

The Body and the Wheel would be performed for five nights during the week preceding Holy Week. The commitment of all fifty members of the cast became obvious when no one groaned as Bill announced our schedule of three weeks of rehearsals. The performers included many families with children as young as five. Dinners and homework would have to take a backseat to rehearsals.

Auditions for *The Body and the Wheel* happened after Mass on the Sunday before Ash Wednesday. Bill told us to celebrate Mardi Gras for all it was worth, because Lent would mean sacrificial work and commitment. Bill took me aside after, and explained that he was going to cast me in the role of Mary. Evidently, he meant it as a compliment, but I told him that I wasn't comfortable playing the Virgin Mary. *How could I play the Virgin Mary after the pain I'd suffered from teaching at the seminary?*

"What do you mean you won't play Mary?"

"Just what I said, Bill. I don't want to play Mary!"

"But, I've already cast all the parts, Ginny!" He quickly searched his notes. "Wait. There's the leper. You can play the leper."

"Okay. Yes, okay. The leper I can play."

Mary! What was he thinking? Mary and I are an ocean apart.

Bill was able to replace me with Ursula Niebuhr. Ursula did not attend Mass at Cranwell, but Bill and I knew her from our theological group. She was Protestant, and one of the first women to receive an advanced theology degree from Oxford University. She was also the widow of the renowned theologian, Reinhold Niebuhr. Ursula and I often enjoyed sharing insights with each other at rehearsals. She introduced me to the idea of envisioning the Holy Spirit as a female figure, Sophia, but she chided me for clinging to the resurrection as a purely physical phenomenon.

The only other performer who was not a member of the Vineyard Community was Spencer Trova, a professional actor who played the role of Jesus. That casting choice was an example of Bill's true theatrical know-how. It allowed the rest of us to come to rehearsal humbled by the actor, reflecting the natural order of things in the play. In the performances, Spencer also stood out from the cast with his charismatic stage presence.

We all soon learned that *The Body and the Wheel* was not a religious pageant play and that although we were a community, this was not your typical "community theater" experience; we had Bill directing and Spencer playing Jesus. Each of us knew the stories in the play by heart, having heard them on Sundays while growing up. Now we craved to know about these biblical characters we were each portraying. "How am I supposed to know what it's like to be possessed by demons?" a man asked one evening, after Bill suggested that his lines sounded flat.

"You will find out. Spend the next week imagining where there may be demons in your life today. If you're playing Pilate, observe politicians on the news or imagine what you would do if you had power. If you're playing Peter, reflect on what makes you passionate."

At home, songs by The Who and Bob Dylan resonated through our house at night. In the mornings, after the girls left for school, I drank my coffee to Barry Manilow and Neil Diamond. I reflected on Bill's direction, "Relive a time in your life, Ginny, when you felt like a leper." *That will be easy.*

The memories flooded me. I was the girl back in Easthampton, afraid and embarrassed by my drunk father. The curate who refused to let me practice birth control, but showed no compassion about my miscarriage. Fr. Gilbert's disgusting revelation. The pain he caused me, which left me numb for months. I'm imprisoned in mind as well as in body.

Then I remembered Liam, as he had stood, sloped shoulders in my office at the seminary, his white cheeks flushed and confiding in me his tortured story of the stick-and-the-shower. The church splits the body of laypeople from their spirit, and does the same with its priests and nuns as it perpetuates celibacy.

I stayed in my room, praying, not aware of the time.

"Mom, it's time to leave for rehearsal." Leslie knocked on my bedroom door. She helped me put on my costume, wrapping the rags around me. Her gentleness was healing. At rehearsal, I felt a vibrancy in my voice as I delivered my line from Matthew, "Lord, if you're willing, you can make me clean."

After each rehearsal, we gathered in a circle around the altar for the Eucharistic prayer. Delivering our lines had been the liturgical reading and the preaching of the Word. When the host was put into my hands, I sensed the fervent desire of Jesus to heal the worst of the wounded.

Flyers hung in the market promoting the upcoming performances of *The Body and the Wheel*. "You must be exhausted with all your rehearsals!" friends and acquaintances declared when we would see them in town. The cast wasn't really exhausted, but we were slowing down in rehearsals, trying to savor the process of exploring the gospel, unwilling to let go of the stories that had captivated us.

George was playing the role of Peter. It was a big part and it took almost an hour to read all his lines. Tierney practiced with him every night, until he learned them all.

The Vineyard Community Performs The Body and the Wheel

"Packed! The chapel is packed!" the woman who washes Jesus' feet whispered to me backstage. The pews accommodated five hundred people. The house was full for all the performances.

My mornings were no longer spent frozen in bed. My routine during those days included cleaning house, preparing my lesson plans, and chatting on the phone with a neighbor until eleven, when I drove to the chapel and knelt in gratitude for the transformation I experienced. Often there were other men and women who had taken a break from work or stopped to pray between errands.

One or two nights during the performances, while alone backstage waiting for my cue to enter, I pondered what had happened. Intuition told me that the transformation, as I called it, had been part of a process, not just an event that happened. During those mornings in bed, I had let the inner truth of those frightening memories become my litany. Later, I learned that many other cast members had gone through their own religious experiences.

As if without warning, it was our final performance. The last scene was always moving. After the crucifixion was portrayed, the lights faded, and the chapel went dark. Spencer slipped backstage. Then, slowly, one faint spotlight came up on Mary Magdalene. "He is risen like he said. He is risen like he said."

As the lights slowly came back up, all the characters, circling the stage before the altar, murmured to one another, "He is risen like he said."

Mary Magdalene moved to the first pew and addressed an audience member, "He is risen as he said." Then Mary of Bethany, followed by each cast member, walked through the aisles, repeating the line to people in the audience.

We were overwhelmed by what had happened to us. The last performance was on the Saturday night before Palm Sunday. Holy Week was a true gift, but as I adhered to the format of church services on Holy Thursday and Good Friday, directions that I'd been following since childhood—stand, sit, and kneel—the ritual felt stiff and inflexible. We're back in the worst of medieval, not the best of gospel, times.

More than a few of us felt let down once the production ended its run. The entire cast gathered to share their experiences. One person suggested that we ask the Jesuits to lead us in a weekend retreat. A tall handsome man with thick white hair stood and spoke. "Wasn't the experience of community and exploring the gospels spiritual enough for you?" Christopher had been a priest until he fell in love and married a former nun. "Getting down on our knees is giving in to tradition. We need to party instead."

And so, Christopher reserved a room in a restaurant and we switched roles to happy party people. I decided to add on a personal retreat for myself as well.

Setting Aside Time for Prayer

I planned to give two hours each morning to my retreat: a half hour for spiritual reading, a half hour for prayer, and an hour of reflective writing.

Whether reading a book on church history passed as spiritual reading, I never asked myself. A seminarian from Queen of Peace had given me a book on Emperor Constantine. I sat on our plaid sofa with bright sun streaming through the windows and was introduced to his vision during battle. Like Christopher, Constantine had bypassed getting down on his knees and praying in order to be a Christian. At his dictate, you became one whether you wanted to or not.

After reading, I moved to an easy chair to pray. Nothing happened after I closed my eyes and offered some words of thanksgiving. Still, I stayed there for my self-dictated half hour. Nothing happened for a week. *Where's God's spirit? Talk to me Jesus.* Disappointed, I put a record on the phonograph to let music lure my soul into prayer. Each day, I listened to my favorite, *Bridge Over Troubled Water.* As Simon and Garfunkel relaxed me, I noticed my heart quickening toward the end of the song when I heard, "Sail on silver girl . . . your time has come . . . " *Jesus, you are my bridge over troubled water.*

One morning in my mind's eye, I saw a long dirt road and in the distance a white-cloaked Jesus walking with some disciples. The next day my vision changed: Jesus was directly before me. His face was only a hand's length away. He spoke only with his eyes, which revealed mercy and affection. I said nothing for the fifteen or twenty minutes we were together. But afterwards, I sensed a wave of the Holy Spirit. It took hold of me.

A new routine came into my life. *Extended prayer every day.*

7

MY FATHER'S LEGACY

Massachusetts, 1973

To greet the new decade that began a few years earlier, I initiated a ritual with the children. On New Year's Eve, George set a fire in the fireplace and I placed a large blank poster board with brightly colored markers on the floor. Each daughter was invited to reflect on the past decade and list one of the best things and one of the worst things that had happened. Leslie started by neatly writing, "John F. Kennedy was assassinated." Katherine followed with, "Martin Luther King was assassinated." Pamela added, "Bobby Kennedy was assassinated." Tierney printed "The War."

Tears stung my eyes as I saw how strife was forming us. As a child during World War II, I had been a fervent patriot. But as the Vietnam War escalated, it became harder to hide behind a flag. George questioned President Kennedy's choice to send military advisers to Vietnam, and now that the "conflict" was actually a war, his objections and anger grew. He and my father always avoided talking about it.

Soon George and I spent our Sundays traveling with the kids to peace demonstrations sponsored by an independent Catholic group. I tutored a student at George's school on how to avoid the draft.

Then in July, I lost my father. He lived to be eighty-three years old, in spite of being a heavy drinker and a three pack-a-day chain smoker. On a Saturday he had a small stroke and went to the hospital in Northampton. On the drive to visit him, memories flooded me. Good and bad.

George had always been very good with Tommy. One afternoon at the hospital, he brought Leslie to visit and he brought the *New York Times*, my father's favorite paper with its cherished crossword puzzle.

"Leslie, go over and look out the window, dear." Her grandfather pointed. She obeyed. "See that park?" She nodded. "That's where I took you for walks in your carriage when you were just a tiny baby."

Leslie turned to him, her eyes full of tears. Just before following George and Leslie from the room, I told him that I had planted oodles of nasturtiums in our rock garden.

"That makes me happy, Virginia. Nasturtiums are good, hardy, old-fashioned plants. We used to plant them in our garden."

I savored that he remembered. Two days later, at ten in the evening, with Tommy's hand putting small letters into little squares, the radiant light in his head was extinguished by a massive assault. I was numb.

His wake was crowded. Not with his relatives. But with folks from the town I had never met. Over and over, one and then another said, "Tommy was my mailman. He'd read aloud in Polish what came for me because I didn't know English then. I'm sorry to see him go." Or it was said, "He'd read it in French."

Tommy hadn't carried mail in more than thirty years, but the church in Easthampton was full. Three Jesuits from Cranwell had offered to preside at the funeral. They picked up Tierney at a drama camp in Stockbridge for the service. Beside me in the pew, after reading Psalm 121 at the lectern, Leslie sobbed and Katherine covered her face with her hands. Pam was in England traveling on a tour lead by a layman who taught at Cranwell. We waited until she came home to tell her about my father.

On the way to the cemetery, Tommy's sister, Aunt Nora, said that if she were able to have such a glorious funeral Mass, she'd be willing to go to heaven tomorrow. But Blanche was not happy about the Jesuits "barging in" on her husband's funeral. She had planned a military burial to honor what she Tommy's service during our country's war in World War II.

My heart was hardened by her insistence on a veteran's burial, which ruined the beauty of the funeral Mass. Right there, next to the ordinary granite stone that marked my grandparents' graves, I listened to volleys shatter the peace of a July sky shifting from gray to blue. *These sounds used to thrill me on Memorial Day and at Fort Devens.* Another rifle barrage. *This is the tenacity of patriotism.* More rifles. A Legionnaire in full dress uniform, with worn, wrinkled skin, ceremonially placed a new, fresh, correctly triangulated American flag into my mother's arms. Another into mine.

All the way home, as we drove up the hills into the Berkshires, my breaths were small inhales, followed by small exhales. Just enough to keep me alive. When we finally pulled into our driveway, I reluctantly carried the stiff, folded flag. I was the first out of our car, first through the living room, into the kitchen, and to the back shed where I lifted the cover of the rubbish bin and thrust the flag of my country against the slop of wet cereal, coffee grounds, and tin cans. I slammed the top over the flag, with a breath as deep as a canyon.

I cried within. *Why do our lives have to be haunted by wars? Never again will I let patriotism break my heart!*

George stood in the doorway. I leaned against him and sobbed for the passing of my father, who, except for three decades of his eighty-three years, was Tommy Sullivan with no active service rank other than that earned by a splendid mind and a caring, loving heart.

Two months after my father was buried, on a visit to my mother with George, I noticed on a metal TV table in the living room a plaque that in raised lettering said Pvt. Thomas Sullivan.

"The U. S. government sent it to me. I want you to put it by the gravestone." Worry had furled itself across Blanche's face since Tommy's death. Her gray hair, grown long, straggled on each side of her thin face.

"Mom, you should go to a beauty parlor and have your hair done."

"Virginia, be serious! We don't have to be ashamed of your father's service in World War I. He was a good soldier."

"Mom. Put it away."

"But the government wants us to put this near the grave. It said so in the letter. You want to see it?"

Blanche's hand shook as she reached for a cigarette and her small, sharp manicure scissors to cut the filter off.

"How can you refuse the federal government?" Her voice sharpened. "It's the law!"

"The law you honor isn't even giving you life insurance and other benefits for his World War I service."

"But that was because of the shame. His officer's rank was stripped." She choked up. "His dishonorable discharge—"

"Exactly. And Mom, look at this awful war our government is waging now."

"Don't you dare start your foolish madness about Vietnam! Cardinal Spellman supports it." Fire suddenly flashed in her dark eyes. "I won't listen to this. Your father brought you up to be patriotic. And I brought you up to respect authority."

"Blanche, Blanche . . . " George bent close to her. Spoke softly as he betrayed me. "Put the plaque in the ground by the grave if you want. Tommy was your husband, so it's your choice."

"He'd want it there, don't you think, George?" Her voice trembled.

"I don't really know, Blanche. But I do know it's your decision to make."

In the car he said, "For God's sake, you're his daughter, but she's his widow."

8

SPRING FORWARD

Lenox, Massachusetts, 1970s

Daylight saving time pushed us forward in the spring. Dusk seemed to start at sunrise and last until starlight. George and I attended a Marriage Encounter Weekend at Shadowbrook, a former Jesuit novitiate near Tanglewood.

The leaders sent us up to bed at eight in the evening, much to our delight as we had so much to share. Enjoying a bottle of wine was romantic, as was making love in a place formerly housed only by celibates. When one husband complained the next morning that being alone with his wife for such a long time without television was a pain, we covered our mouths to hide our smiles.

Unfortunately the joy and sense of community that we had created in the Berkshires would be coming to an end, after seven years. Many private schools in the area were suffering from low enrollment due to the poor economy. The private schools in Lenox began closing, and George received a letter from the headmaster at Windsor Mountain, announcing that it was shutting down. After he read it, he handed the letter to me. He couldn't even say it aloud.

He sat down next to me on the sofa, his shoulders slumped, his face haggard. "We can't afford one daughter in college and two more going next year."

"I'm sure one of the kids will get a scholarship. And our school's not the only one hitting the rocks." I smiled and tried to put a lighter note on what loomed ahead as a disaster.

"We might as well shoot for the moon." George put an arm around me. "What do you want to do with the rest of your life? You've supported me in all my life changes . . . moved to new places for my career. Now it's your turn."

In spite of the tiredness in his eyes, his voice was tender and caring. "What's your heart's desire?"

"Study for another master's?" I mumbled, staring out the window.

"Yes. George Albert had said that you belong in a theology school. The school in Cambridge."

Fr. George Albert was a professor at Cranwell and the leader of our Vineyard Community. He had urged me to get a Master's Degree in Divinity. *"Let your spirit develop and soar, while you study."* That's what George had said.

"Weston. It's called the Weston Jesuit School of Theology." My eyes welled with tears. "But, that's crazy! I have to look for another teaching job and it would be a two-hour commute!"

"You've got a calling, a destiny. You're enrolling at Weston. Money be damned!"

Thus, we embarked on the greatest risk of our lives, trusting in God.

Cranwell School and the Vineyard Community Close
The following Sunday held more bad news. After Mass at Cranwell, George Albert sadly announced that Cranwell was closing. Also, the

provincial was insisting that the chapel be closed and the Vineyard Community "shut down."

I managed to contain my anger and disappointment until we got in the car to drive home, but before George even put the key in the ignition, I let it out.

"The provincial? The provincial! Well, this is one provincial who won't wrap me around his little finger like the one in New Hampshire tried to do! I'll show him."

"Is a provincial like a pope?" one of the kids asked from the back seat.

"Time will tell," George mumbled. "Let's see what happens at the meeting this week."

Even Mother Nature refused to cooperate, shipping the Berkshires a winter storm on the day of our regular weekly Vineyard Community meeting, which was led by Fr. Albert.

"No one will come," Fr. Albert proclaimed to his first arrivals, George and me. But come they did, stamping snow off their boots and shaking it from their scarves. They came in droves, some incredulous, some sad, some determined that, when the school closed, the chapel and Vineyard Community would not. If the school was in demise, efforts had to be made to retain the property.

My task in the campaign to save the Vineyard was to write letters to the New England Jesuit provincial and beg for lasting life for the Vineyard. I also sent proposals to Bishop Medeiros on utilizing the property as a retreat house and conference center. These missives included reports detailing the success of the Vineyard and its ability to expand the Catholic community within the Berkshires. At the closure of one report, I even wrote, "I don't know if I'm Judith or Esther, I only know that the Vineyard can't die."

The Jesuits did send someone wonderful to the Vineyard. Fr. Jerry Finnegan became the pastoral and liturgical leader, replacing the

Jesuits who had served before. Charley, George, Dick, and Ed were sent off to new teaching assignments, one by one, dreading to leave us, as much as we dreaded to see them go.

Fortunately, Tanglewood saved us that summer with its beauty. After the last graduations and the schools permanently closed, we would take the whole family, lie on blankets, and savor the concerts. We found them almost prayerful.

Then came fall and a swarm of good-byes to our older daughters as they headed off to college. George and I took Leslie to Holy Cross in Worcester, drove Pamela to Goucher in Maryland, and brought Katherine to Logan Airport, where she flew to California to attend the University of Pacific.

Bills greeted us when we got home, but there was also an envelope with no return address. Inside was over $200 cash, in small bills Every other week envelopes continued to arrive. We savored the generosity and affection that it signified, as well as the money itself. The senders, whom we suspected were from the Vineyard, reminded us of how fragile our hearts felt.

George never flagged from his search for a job, and I enrolled in a course at Weston, the theology school, just two blocks from Harvard Square. Early on in the semester, I was fortunate to meet Fr. Brian McDermott, who tutored me. Although I already had undergraduate and graduate degrees, those were in English and Education.

Brian gave me a book on Christology. "Read the first two chapters and then write a commentary."

It's going to take me two hours just to translate this theological language into English. Should my commentary be in English, theological speak, or Latin?

9

A JOURNEY BEGINS

Cambridge, Massachusetts, Late 1970s

Moving again. Second year of studying at
Weston Jesuit School of Theology.

Easing the sadness of our last day in the Berkshires, many of our
generous friends from the Vineyard Community helped us move from
our house in Lenox to an apartment in a two-family house in Belmont,
a suburb next to Cambridge. The realtor who had found us the apartment told me a bus stop was only a block away. "Oh, we never take the
bus," I explained.

"You will," she replied. She knew the crowded roads and non-
existent parking in Cambridge and Boston. Fortunately, the theology
school was only a fifteen-minute ride on the bus.

We had left the Berkshires, but the Vineyard did not leave us. In
my first semester, I observed a large exhibit space at the library shared
by Weston and the Episcopal Divinity School, that was unused. This
would be perfect to hang John and Primm's art from the Vineyard
community. Surprised by the quick acceptance when I showed the
head of the library photos of creative arts pieces from the Vineyard,

I arranged for our community to hang vestments, butterflies, stars, banners, and an altar cloth with its purple grapes. It brightened the theological library with living faith.

On a table near the entry to the library was a book for comments. I sometimes stood to greet visitors, many of whom were surprised that a local community with only sixty families could express themselves through creativity.

"Do they intend to evangelize?" A priest asked me.

"Oh, no. That never crosses their minds."

"Well it does give witness. We should get every parish to do that!"

If I only had the time, but I still have to get through my first semester.

Soon after moving to Belmont, Tierney was confirmed in our local parish. As part of preparation for that coming of age ritual, parents were invited by the religious Sisters leading the program to an evening of reflection in the parish hall where we gathered in small groups at round tables.

When we arrived, parents were invited to reflect in silence for ten minutes on who Jesus was for us. We had not been assigned seats, but as it happened the women and men sat at separate tables. When my table was asked to share our reflections, our responses centered on how we encountered Jesus in the loving and healing presence in the Eucharistic celebrations at Mass, in prayer, and in our ongoing everyday lives. Beside me was a table with four fathers. None said a word for awhile. Finally one spoke. "I thought that Jesus Christ was the Second Person of the Blessed Trinity. There is the Father, the Son and the Holy Spirit."

The other three men agreed. *Isn't that a pre-Vatican II sensibility? That approach is considered 'high Christology.' Placing Jesus at a remote and abstract level. Since the women experienced their relationship with Jesus through the human qualities of Jesus, I guess that puts us in the category of 'low Christology .'*

The day I started my second semester at Weston, I walked up three flights and peered into every room. *Hmmm. Tweed jackets, cardigan sweaters, white shirts with ties. They're all priests, but not one Roman collar!* But as a married woman and mother in this celibate stronghold, I was out of place, and I still had not been accepted into the master's degree program.

Fr. Gus sat behind a desk with a sign, Admissions Office, on it. His face was kind, his voice was kind, his message was not.

"You see, Virginia, you never spent a day in any parochial school or Catholic college. And, well, another problem is your age. I believe you are in your early forties?"

"I'm not sure why that matters?"

"And you may not be up to reading long assignments and writing serious papers. The brain cells die as we age."

"Father, I had excellent grades from four courses I took here last semester."

"Yes, well, you're a *layperson*. It would be easier if you were a nun."

I left the building and crossed the street to sit on a bench in the Radcliffe Yard. A layperson. *Why is there so much prejudice against people! Aren't we part of the Church? Aren't most of the people in God's Church laypeople?*

Irritation propelled me off the bench, across the road, and up the stairs of the Weston building to Brian, who had tutored me the previous semester, and was now my informal advisor. As soon as he heard the impediments to my acceptance, he jumped from his chair and raced down the stairs to the admissions desk. I hovered nearby, but smiled when I heard him say, "For God's sake, Gus, she reads Kierkegaard as recreational material."

Well, it was true, but only because I was fascinated by the Danish philosopher's leap-of-faith point of view and resistance to his denomination. It was so intense that when he was dying he'd accept Communion only from a lay believer.

The next week I got a letter of acceptance into the Master's of Divinity program with a generous scholarship.

My father, Tommy Sullivan,
in his mailman's uniform.

My mother, Blanche Bernadette
Boothillitte, holding me at
our home in Easthampton.

My mother and I on the day
of my First Communion.

High School portrait.

Waitressing on Cape Cod in the summer.

February 27, 1954

With our parents, Tommy and Blanche on the left and
Stanley and Jane on the right.

We were married for 49 years, until George's passing.

Taking care of the girls.

The whole family, with my father
holding Tierney.

John and Primm ffrench designed art installations, which were made by members of the Vineyard Community, and then hung on the back wall of Pierce Chapel. Stars for Christmas.

Butterflies for Easter.

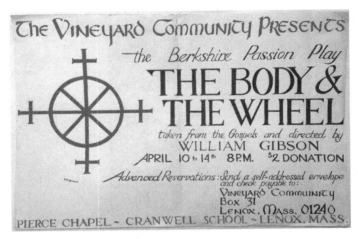

Poster, designed by Primm ffrench, for The Body and
The Wheel. The play was written and directed by
William Gibson for the Vineyard Community.

NCR article on The Body and The Wheel. From
left Bill, George and Bill Fessler.

Graduating from Weston
Jesuit School of Theology.

On retreat with Weston students
and faculty at Eastern Point Retreat House in Gloucester.

Gathering of colleagues at a National
Association of Lay Ministers event.

Receiving and honorary degree from Elms College.

Preaching

Vacationing in Arizona.

In Ireland during our whirlwind tour of Europe.

Relaxing in Leslie's home in Vermont, shortly after George's
stroke with Tierney and all our grandchildren. In the front
Tara, Andy, and Ryan and in the back Renee and Nicole.

My grandchildren dancing in my home in the Berkshires.
From left Andy, Ryan, Renee, and Tara

Three generations of women, at a family celebration at Tierney's home. From from left Tierney, Nicole, Tara , Leslie, Pam, and Renee.

10

BLENDING THEOLOGY,
SPIRITUALITY, AND MINISTRY

Cambridge and Boston, Massachusetts, Late 1970s

Courses at Weston Jesuit School of Theology,
Harvard University, and Boston University.

Theology

Through the Boston Theological Institute, students from the Weston Jesuit School of Theology could enroll in courses at five other schools in the area. I quickly signed up for The Interpretation of Religious Experience because it was taught by H. Richard Niebuhr, the brother-in-law of my friend Ursula. He assigned us Rudolf Otto's book, *The Idea of the Holy*, and I fell in love.

Otto's concept of *mysterium tremendum et fascinans*, which describes what some feel during worship or prayer, lured me into wanting to know more. He claimed that no matter what we might experience, our belief system piles what we should believe on top of it. By noticing our feelings, especially when apart from worship, we can sense a glimmer of a message. I based my paper for this course on an inquiry into the spiritual lives of worshipers in the Vineyard Community. When I saw the A+ on the graded paper, I wished that my father could see my success. *Now I just might get a Divinity master's degree!*

Practicum on the Sacraments

The other exciting course was Sacraments, which was held one weekend a month in a nearby retreat house. Saturday featured lectures on the sacraments and Sunday was the practicum. The first weekend featured baptism, which in an emergency, lay believers can perform. Each student held a baby doll and named her.

Of course, as a woman, I was not permitted to participate hands-on in the sessions on the sacraments of reconciliation, holy orders, or Eucharist. Instead, I cried in my room. *You got it wrong, God, not ordaining your women!* With my head down, I spilled anguished tears that soaked the bedspread.

Pastoral Counseling

During that semester, another course was Pastoral Counseling in which we paired up with another student to share our experiences each week. I was assigned to work with Phil, a fine, serious seminarian, who listened to me after I listened to him. Then we each wrote summaries of what we heard and how we responded.

The class sessions were more challenging, though I was pleased that the course was taught by a nun, Sr. Claire, as well as a Jesuit priest.

One day the priest asked us, "Can you get mad at God?"

Not one hand was raised. He walked up to a male student. "How about it? Can you get mad at God?"

The student blushed but said nothing. The professor continued. "What's the matter? You don't think God could take it?"

"No, it just doesn't seem right." His voice was low.

"Maybe God will turn on you and wipe you out?"

The air was electric in the class and we left charged up with questions of our own. *This is good. He's preparing us to handle the challenges that are to come.*

Atheism

I had no trouble reading Freud and others who challenged a belief in faith. What startled me were the upsets of some of the other students. One young nun said in a frightened voice, "What would I ever do if I came face to face with an atheist? I'd be so upset I wouldn't know what to say."

How are you going to share your faith if you're scared to talk to nonbelievers? I knew plenty in the Berkshires. They are human beings just like us.

Human Sexuality

The difficult class was Human Sexuality. It was taught by Fr. Paul and another priest. *Both of these people are celibate. They may have doctorates, but what does either of them really know about sexuality?*

What the priests did know were the church rules. "No young adults should ever live together before marriage." *Young adults don't always obey their parents. Do you think they'll listen to a celibate priest?* But I silenced my own questions and observations during each class and felt heaviness in my heart and a headache when I left.

The Church's absolute silence on these practical issues of sexuality made it worse. How can a celibate advise or sympathize with a woman in her cycle? The past week one priest told me that he was conflicted about birth control. *Rome's policy on marriage is archaic, authoritarian, and inflexible. Of course you're conflicted!* But I didn't reply, because I was afraid I might start screaming.

Clinical Pastoral Ministry

In addition to the academic courses, completing a Master's in Divinity included participation in a hands-on pastoral program. I enrolled in Clinical Pastoral Education, sponsored by Andover Newton Theological School. A hospital setting needed to be secured. I visited Massachusetts General Hospital, but was told, "You don't wear a religious order habit or a clerical collar? You're not suitable for this hospital. Perhaps you can find a doctor's clinic that will take you."

University Hospital in another part of Boston did accept me. The first few days, the students gathered together as a group for instruction. We were to lock our pocketbooks, wear a blazer, keep tissues and change in our pockets, and introduce ourselves as chaplain. We were to visit all nine wards and meet patients with different illnesses. Each week we would meet with our supervisor, a Methodist minister with decades of experience in hospital chaplaincy. Before each meeting we had to submit a verbatim, a transcription of a conversation with a patient.

Needless to say I flunked my first supervision when he read my verbatim.

He barked at me, "Did you say, 'Hi. I'm Ginny?' Is that how you actually introduced yourself? From now on say, 'Good morning, I'm Chaplain Finn.' You are a professional and you have to act like it. You're not a friendly neighbor."

I quickly realized that the patients needed me. Sitting beside a terminally ill older woman, I listened as she told me that her husband calls her each night, asking her how soon she's going to die. "He's sick of waiting for it to happen. It's too hard on him," she said.

I was humbled. I took her hand and told her that it's not God saying that to her.

There were lighter moments. One patient told his doctor that whenever I was working, I should come sit with him. I was surprised, because Harold had never seemed religious. On one of my visits with him, I gently brought God up.

"Harold, you never mention God."

"Did you say you have a dog?"

"No, I asked you about God."

"Spell it backwards, it's dog. Don't mention the other word."

That afternoon, a married woman, about to be discharged, didn't want to go home and face debts caused by her husband's terrible gambling habit. In her eyes I saw a glint of anger.

"What would you like to do when you see your husband?" I asked.

"Give him a swift kick in the ass!"

Holding back a smile, I clutched her hand.

"Oh my God!" She mumbled. "I never could say that to a priest. But it feels good to get if off my chest to you."

She never knew what a gift she was to me. *For some patients I might serve as salve, not substitute.*

One nun in a habit doing the chaplaincy program liked to say to me, "You're so insightful, Virginia, it's hard to believe that you're a layperson." She actually referred to me as Sister Virginia.

Before I knew it, my studies were completed and it was time to start my thesis, but it was taking me months to discover an acceptable topic.

I discovered Friedrich von Hügel, a lay theologian, who died in 1925 and was said by the Church to be tainted by modernism. He was a spiritual director, a husband, and a father. If von Hügel had a fault, it was that he wrote extensively long sentences that a reader had to work out, but the working out was worth it. He actually wrote of perceiving a divorce between theology and spirituality because the institutional Church relied only on discursive and abstract thought and neglected intuitive values. Von Hügel brought delight at times. For example, when he wrote about the differences between *"isness"* and *"oughtness."*

Isness and Oughtness. When oughtness dominates isness, the person disappears. When isness overwhelms oughtness, the self becomes God.

George was convinced that I deserved a long vacation to celebrate the end of my studies, and that my thesis topic would come to me during our journey. It would certainly give me time to mull over *isness* and *oughtness.*

We planned a six-week vacation–destination, Stockton, California, a place we had never seen, but where our twin daughters were graduating from college. Although it meant missing several weeks of school, we were taking Tierney and her innumerable class assignments.

My deserved reputation as Last Minute Minnie meant spending the day, and into the night, before our trip packing, unpacking, and repacking, unaware of how our journey might pay off. Will this trip be fruitful? Is it the intention of the Holy Spirit to traverse so far from my responsibilities?

Crossing the whole U. S. of A. by automobile meant having space in the car to bring the twins and their belongings back home to Boston. Is that too optimistic? Five people and college stuff?

During the packing, I remembered von Hugel's letter to his niece about preparing for a trip. The memory meant I squandered time looking for a book of his writings, which I hid in a duffle bag as if it were a forbidden bottle of whiskey. I hugged the volume before camouflaging it. Even though he died in 1925 I loved von Hugel, the lay Catholic theologian, memorialized by Yeats, the spiritual director of Evelyn Underhill, an Anglican, one of the many who befriended von

Hugel, under Vatican suspicion for being a lay theologian and friend of those accused of that evil 'Modernism.'

Hadn't I spent the whole year worrying, praying, and weeping about how foolhardy it had been to sell our home in the Berkshires and hike off to Boston for this M. Div. Degree? And what would be the fruit of that? Four years of studying scripture, systematics, spirituality, and pastoral counseling could leave me by the wayside in Harvard Square while I most likely, would return to teaching remedial reading. By the Atlantic, Boston had a seafood restaurant called No Name. I no longer feasted there because I now called myself No Name who dares to keep her foot in the church door and minister.

At home George said go wherever you can get a ministry job, anywhere in the country. I'll come along. I can get a job. On campus I told professors and fellow students that, of course, I had to find something in Boston where George was working. I couldn't ask him to move, again.

God waited till the week before we left on our adventure, to whisper that He didn't care where I went or what I did. He'd be with me.

Warren, Ohio, is not Manhattan or Boston. Still it was our last taste of urban life until Denver. What none of us knew about geography was that our land is mostly endless with only flat fields of wheat and corn to guarantee that we weren't on Mars.

"People don't live here," Tierney said every half hour.

"Somebody is planting these fields," George countered. "But it sure as hell isn't New England where we have places named Land's End. Here it's nothing but endless land." As usual, her father's jokes brightened her day and appeased her.

When not driving or dozing, I spread myself across the back seat to work on the thesis. This jaunt's blessing was that George and Tierney were so bored that they asked me to read some of my thesis notes on how culture influenced the religious experience of lay people in 15th century Germany, particularly in Bavaria. Quickly, I came across a bit of religious history they might find intriguing and read:

"In Bavaria the hunt was an important activity so it's not surprising that as devotion to the Eucharist intensified, it was felt that the Host could best be honored by what was already respected in local everyday context. Consequently, doors were widened in churches to allow laymen to ride elaborately dressed horses down the main aisle. Then they genuflected before the Host or the richly designed tabernacle. The equines were blessed by a priest with holy water before their entrance. In 1490, there were 7,055 horses who participated in what was called the Holy Blood Umritt."

"Wow!" exclaimed Tierney. "That would never be allowed today. Even on the St. Francis feast, when the dogs and cats and people's parakeets are blessed, it's always done outside church."

"See, the Vatican does change some things." George sighed then brightened. "Ah, a place to stop for lunch."

But once I'd started sharing my discoveries, lunch didn't stop me. "You see, according to Blondel, a French philosopher, what is divine has to be given in a form which allows us humans to enter into it. But, once that happens, it becomes part of a natural order, and is subject to its determinations."

"Can we please just eat our lunch?" George countered.

Tierney quickly chimed in, "Yeah, Mom."

The flatland journey did not draw me into prayer, but I noticed a contemplative attitude softening my spirit. At times I just murmured to myself phrases from von Hugel's writings. 'God is the Seeker and the Sought; each of us is a Seeker and is Sought.'

Four star restaurants are non-existent on the Midwest's big belly. Instead we ate at the identical, no-star, rest stop gas stations that lined the route. Tierney inevitably ordered a local dish, but half way through the meal said, "Oh, I wish I'd ordered what you did, Dad. It looks much yummier than mine."

The exchange of plates with no word from her dad symbolized his particular brand of generosity. As did, after she'd fallen asleep in that night's motel, his request that I read him my section on marriage published in a Jesuit Studies journal. To not wake Tierney on the cot, I whispered 'The unity of coupling emerges from the bonding that grew within us in childhood. This may account for why the bonding sense reverberates with strength in cultures and cannot be avoided. We bring this 'sense' with us to adulthood and experience it in our cultural mores. That is why 'oneness' is implied in sexual sharing. Because of the depth of the physicality and the affectivity, each spouse may experience a new freedom through unity."

"I can't believe they published this! Of course, it's all very relevant. It's essential that priests and sisters know what happens in marriage. How can they minister without this information? Now, keep reading, honey, it's very stimulating."

"George, did you forget about Tierney?"

"Tomorrow night we're getting her a separate room."

When we finally reached the Rocky Mountains it was succulent. We traversed up the gang plank roads that I was certain on every hairpin turn intended to plunge us into ancient stones a mile drop off the road. But we made it to Salt Lake City and picked up George's mother to join us. After going through the desert of Reno, I savored the splurge of the greenway that was ushering us toward Lake Tahoe.

Suddenly everything sped by and soon we were greeted by Kerry and Pam. They had a multitude of friends from abroad, who were also graduating from Elbert Covell College. Part of the University of the Pacific, the school intentionally twinned American students, who had to be fluent in Spanish for acceptance, with foreign students learning English in dorms and classes. One moment an Islamic student from Bangladesh was telling me he liked the symbols and paintings in a Catholic church as he sometimes found himself bored while praying in a mosque. The next moment a Venezuelan student asked me if I was as knowledgeable in Spanish as my daughters.

A quiet break came during the graduation ceremony and brought with it the sad awareness that the past was dying at the feet of the present. In church I savored it happening; in family I mourned it. My twins graduating from college, Leslie soon to be married, and Tierney midway through high school.

The California sun was burning on us; trees surrounding the park rustled but no breeze fanned my cheeks. With a slight limp Pam crossed the stage to receive her degree. No cast, no brace, no crutches. I saw in my mind the day she threw away her crutches and hobbled at a run across the lawn to join friends.

With my own degree almost in hand, I was learning, like Pam, to live without a crutch. Time for the real world again. Please, God, let me use my degree, for ministry.

After the post-graduation party which included many tissues wiping eyes as the graduates, including our own two, gave farewell hugs to friends who were not leaving for different parts of our country, but leaving our country for their homelands, we went to the dorm to load up and weigh down the car with an inventory of collegiate belongings. Then off to San Francisco and dinner.

At a round table in a Chinese restaurant, George exulted in his role as Pater Familias. His face agleam with pride and pleasure as he twirled the lazy Susan with Asian dishes around to his each of us.

The next morning while George brought his mother to the airport, I was at the motel, repacking my own luggage. I tucked my thesis and the von Hugel books deep into the bottom. My celebratory feeling finally broke through. Anticipatory joy filled my spirit for our return trip. Weeks ahead without thought or theology. Weeks ahead without church folderol. Weeks ahead without needs or duties. Weeks ahead without cooking or cleaning.

The country was as wide as we traveled toward home as it was when we traveled from home. A week later when we hit Texas, I felt a tickle on my shoulder from Tierney's curls and heard her whisper, "Vastness. It's the vastness of it all." before she fell back.

I savored the insight. Our country was vast, a quality I embraced for its soothing gift of splendor and spaciousness. The vastness of God's creation revealed a sense of God's glory, above all, greater than all. Yet, by the time Smokey Mountain National Park appeared on the horizon, all of us were so satiated by scenery that phrases of appreciation sounded scripted. "Almost there!" George proclaimed as we approached Washington D.C.

Inside myself I felt a sense of completion, having experienced our country inch by inch, the northern and the southern routes. Within the vastness I had sensed God's transcendence–mysterium tremendum. A rector at Trinity Episcopal Church in Boston had written a book entitled Your God Is Too Small. My God isn't too small. I had been dealing, in spiritual direction and hospital pastoral care, with God's immanence, God's presence in prayer and in ongoing life experience. This journey revealed a significant dimension of God I had neglected.

From the motel in D.C. I called Leslie and discovered that Church had put a crimp in her wedding plans.

"In order to be married in a church we were supposed to give notice months ago. But we're still going to get married…in a forest in the Berkshires."

I'm sure she heard my gasp through the phone. I tried to process all my thoughts. Why didn't she wait for me to get home to decide this? When will the Church catch up to the world and sanctify a mass outside? Not in time for this wedding. Doesn't the Vatican know that God is present in nature?

"But, don't worry, Mom. It will have a Catholic element. Fr. Hallen has offered to be there and we have a friend who is a Methodist minister. So Fr. Hallen can concelebrate with him."

"Okay…Umm.. When did all this happen? I thought you'd wait for me to come back so we could plan it together–"

"Yes, you're definitely included in the planning. I need you to make a picnic for the reception…We'll need a lot of food for all the guests. And it needs to be vegetarian. Remember, Jeff's a vegetarian. Please hurry home!"

Yes, We'll hurry. But you can call your grandmother and tell her all this.

Leslie's change in plans did bring a wedding day of sunlight, a bride beautiful, and a vegetarian reception I'd prepared which pleased everyone. Except my mother, who kept asking, "When are we going to the church? When are they getting married?"

Training in Spiritual Direction

Shortly after our trip, I arranged through Weston to train as a spiritual director and was the first layperson ever accepted at CRD, the Center for Religious Development in Cambridge. There was a transformative intensity to the process. One hour every week, I would meet individually with each of my eight clients who were coming for spiritual direction. This was followed by writing the session verbatim, attending a weekly session with my supervisor to go over the verbatim, gathering with the other CRD students in training to reflect on the process, and reading books on spirituality and spiritual direction.

At CRD, I witnessed an evolving spiritual growth in my clients. They were invited to openly share where they were with God. *Few lay believers get this opportunity.* They had a striking diversity, even those who were vowed religious.

When I mentioned God, no one actually said "I'd rather talk about dogs," but one man always used "The Force," instead of God. The man shared with me that in the parish his family attended as a child, there had been a priest who was a sexual predator. He could not, because of that, say the word God.

Our supervisor led a discussion on speaking with God. Asking an older nun if God had ever spoken to her, she cried, "No! What would I say? And I don't think I want him speaking to me."

A younger nun, on the other hand, listened for God's personal word or nudge and often received a response.

Fondness for particular seekers sometimes emerged and was always brought to my supervisor's attention through the verbatim. One woman who met with me was studying for a Master's in Divinity at Boston University. She was my age and married.

"I want to be closer to God." Her voice had strength. "For us to be intimate."

"You want to be closer to God." *What exactly does she mean by intimate?* I remembered my training. When a director is unsure of what to say, repeat what you have just heard.

"No! No, I don't want to be closer to God." She had a surprised, anxious look on her face.

"You don't," I simply replied.

"No, because of God's will." She looked at her clenched hands. "To be close to God means having to obey his will. I'm not up to that."

When I suggested she might already be following God's will by studying for a ministerial degree, she was somewhat mollified. When her session had finished, I sat in silence for fifteen minutes as spiritual directors are trained to do. A Vineyard Jesuit, other priests, friends, and George all had told me that I had a calling, a destiny. *Is that God's will?*

No. The obsession to fulfill God's will dominates too many spiritual lives for too many believers. It gets in the way of your relationship with God. In my mind and heart I substituted God's desire, which evokes God's love and a more ready response from the heart.

By the end of the year, I examined the variety of ministries that can come from God's desire. The *blessed* variety is what God encounters within us. *The fascinating marvel of it all. I've found my calling.*

11

LAWS OF SILENCE: BERNARD LAW SEXUAL ABUSE IN THE CATHOLIC CHURCH

Washington, D.C. and the Berkshires, 1975 Meetings in preparation for the Bishops' Bicentennial celebration

In anticipation of the country's birth, the American bishops planned to convene their own Bicentennial in 1976 and incorporate a "democratic outreach" as part of it. There would be writing committees on a number of different topics and a report for each would be presented at the Church's Bicentennial celebration in Detroit. David O'Brien, a professor at the College of the Holy Cross in Worcester and an active leader in the Catholic Peace Fellowship, invited me to join the Personhood Writing Committee. The committee would deal with sexuality and other topics.

I accepted and found myself on a plane to Washington, D.C., and stayed at a convent by the Chesapeake Bay. As I walked into our meeting room, I noticed people at a table shaded by stunning flora beyond the window. There were a couple of Roman collars, including Bishop Bernard Law* of the Springfield-Cape Girardeau Diocese of Missouri.

As I found a place at the table, I was handed a sheaf of papers and told they were results of town meetings held in many dioceses across the country. What startled me was not the discussion, but the papers themselves. I fingered the tiny holes on each side, the first computer printouts I had ever seen. It seemed my Church was moving into present day, as the Second Vatican Council had promised. I wasn't really listening to the others until a voice was raised, that of David's, who was pointing out that the overwhelming consensus of the laity was the Church's need to change its ban on birth control.

Bishop Law's response was immediate. "Put all those papers in the file. Go on to the next question."

"But we haven't discussed these printouts," observed a nun reviewing a handful.

"If these laypeople don't believe in the authority of the magesterium to ban birth control, then they're not Catholics. Go on to the next question."

During our coffee breaks, Law revealed a sociability. To put that together with his abrupt authoritarianism in response to certain issues sparked my curiosity, until later in the day when the committee had moved to a round table for lunch and a few moments of relaxation.

In a casual way, a diocesan seminary priest from the Midwest described a problem regarding a few seminarians who claimed to be heterosexual while studying at their seminary, yet after ordination were active homosexuals.

"It's hard to know whether we should crack down with more effort while they're in the seminary, because it's much harder to monitor behavior after ordination."

A fist slammed down on the table, startling me. The fist belonged to Law who rigidly and angrily proclaimed, "There is not one single homosexual priest in the entire United States. Never refer to that topic again!"

That silenced the table. Unsure about what *was* a safe topic, we found ourselves almost mute, approaching each agenda item with an eye and an ear out for how our "leader" might respond. The safest route was to let Law initiate.

When Law left to attend an important function with the Cardinal of D.C., we wallowed in defeat until David, a committee member who mysteriously knew Bishop Law's calendar, made a suggestion. He could plan our next meeting when Law was traveling to Rome. "Let's see what we come up with without him."

When I returned home after my trip, George reveled in my sharing the story. "While the cat was away did the mice play? Maybe you could invite Alfred Kinsey, he's a new sex expert. More people listen to him than to their parish priest. Imagine Kinsey meeting with Bishop Law."

I had offered to arrange our secretive meeting in the Berkshires, at the National Shrine of Divine Mercy and the Marian Helpers Center. A priest from the Midwest exclaimed, "Norman Rockwell's hometown! What could be more American than to plan for the Bishops' Bicentennial in Norman Rockwell's hometown?"

A few months later we gathered in Stockbridge, without Bishop Law. The rural beauty was relaxing to everyone. While brainstorming, one of the sisters on the committee shared her thoughts. "We must affirm the beauties of sexuality. Emphasize that married love, enacted in bed, is the highest form of intimacy, always and every time revealing a passion that is the heart of spiritual life. Don't you agree, Virginia?"

Hmmm. "Every time." Not so sure about that.

"Yes, Sister. But, let's be realistic in these discussions. Sometimes "married love" is terrific, but sometimes it's just . . . nice."

Is that a quizzical look or a disappointed look on her face? "You see, it can also be inconvenient, given the Church's opinion on birth control," I quietly added.

David, who was a happily married man with four children, nodded in agreement. One of the priests promptly interjected, "'Terrific' is not a suitable adjective to put in the report. I think we should each write our own report, send it to David, and let him put it together."

* Cardinal Bernard Law was part of the hierarchy at the center of the sexual abuse scandal within the Church. He was responsible for moving priests from parish to parish and for covering-up instances of sexual abuse. The following information regarding Cardinal Law was collected from the *National Catholic Reporter, Commonweal Magazine, The Pilot, The Boston Globe,* and *The New York Times.*

January 11, 1984: Bishop Law was appointed by Pope John Paul II to be the archbishop of the Boston Archdiocese, which had two million Roman Catholics. Later that year, Archbishop Law received a letter from a bishop, expressing concerns about the abusive behavior of a priest in his diocese.

May 25, 1985: Archbishop Law was elevated to Cardinal by Pope John Paul II.

July 2001: Cardinal Law admitted that he had received letters which outlined allegations of child molestations, and that he had reassigned these priests to other parishes, despite these allegations.

January 9, 2002: Cardinal Law apologized to victims of abuse in a press conference. (Many priests were later convicted of indecent assault and battery of children.)

April 2002: Cardinal Law attempted to resign his position as Archbishop of Boston, but Pope John Paul II rejected his resignation.

December 9, 2002: In a letter signed by 58 priests, Cardinal Law was implored to resign his post as archbishop.

December 13, 2002: Cardinal Law resigned as Archbishop of Boston.

May 2004: Pope John Paul II appointed Cardinal Law as arch-priest of the Patriarchal Basilica of St. Mary Major, one of the four largest basilicas in Rome.

12

CHAPLAINCY AT MIT

Massachusetts Institute of Technology, Cambridge, 1980s

Red letter days are to be cherished. I received three items in the morning mail—a notice that my piece on sexuality was published in *Studies in the Spirituality of Jesuits*, a notice that I was to be a lay adviser to the National Council of Catholic Bishops (NCCB) Committee on the Laity, and an appointment to the Catholic chaplain's staff at MIT.

Before starting the campus ministry position, I attended two conferences. One was with George in Washington, D.C.: The Religious Leaders Consultation for the World Conference of the United Nations. There I had to deal with George, rather than the world. He was upset that some women leaders referred to the Holy Spirit as feminine.

When I began at MIT, it was suggested that I attend a world conference that included religion in a conversation. The head of the World Conference of Churches complained that the media paid too much attention to the Vatican.

Early in the first semester at MIT, I heard an address by Jerome Weiner, the retiring president, who expressed a negative attitude that surprised me. He charged that it was difficult to lead, because the departments got their own funding from corporations and government.

Especially concerned about nuclear bomb proliferation, Weiner claimed our country needed only one bomb, in case of response if we were attacked.

At MIT, armed with this global vision, I was brought down to earth when my boss, Fr. Robert, told me that he had never worked with a woman before and said, "I think it will be interesting and good for the students who now include more females."

That first semester I discovered how much the students needed prayers and support for the price they paid to succeed at such a prestigious place. "I haven't slept a wink for four nights," one junior confessed. "Glued to the lab. That's why I haven't been at any Advent services. But I must pass my courses, even if I die before Christmas."

"Are you saying that research is suicidal?"

"Yes! Nice way to put it. Give me a lavish funeral now that suicide's no sin."

One of my ministerial tasks was to sit at a table in the coffee shop at the student union and invite students whom I'd seen at Mass to 'chat' about their faith. I did that. The students were polite. When I asked the faith question, each replied that he or she liked the chapel and the folk group that lead the singing. My training at the hospital and in the spiritual direction practicum was to listen. I did that. And I was treated with interesting stories about practical science like how Saran Wrap was first invented; how radar during World War II caused birds to be fried, which led to the creation of microwave ovens; and how the nuclear reactor next to the campus worked.

Ministering to the freshmen was almost the hardest. I shouldn't have been surprised one morning when a student rushed in, didn't sit down, but asked, "Do you have a book about what I'm supposed to believe? I want to be a good Catholic."

"Okay, What's your name? How about you sit and we can talk for a few minutes."

"I'm Kyle. Why do I need to sit down?"

"I'd like to hear what you believe. There are different ways to have faith in God."

"I don't have time for that. I have a meeting with my advisor to select a second major. Just recommend a good book and I'll believe whatever it tells me to believe."

At home I whined to George, evidently quite often. For all the brilliance they had for academics, they where immature in many ways.

"Last week one student called and asked to make an appointment. He had a 'real' dilemma. When we met, his dilemma was that a science fiction movie he wanted to see was opening at the same time as the Mass to celebrate the Immaculate Conception, a holy day of obligation. Would it be okay if he missed mass."

"Well, he probably wants to go the to Star Wars movie. It's opening this weekend. Did you tell him it's not really a dilemma, because he's at M.I.T. and it could be considered part of his professional studies?"

"Oh, George, you're missing my point!"

"Probably. By the way I'm taking Tierney and her friends to see it on Saturday. They announced on the news that it's the end of the series. Too bad you can't come. *You* already have an obligation."

Some of the grad students did want to have meaningful conversations. Caroline, a student whom I really liked, had been married over the summer. But she came to me very upset.

"Chaplain Finn, I need to tell you that before the wedding, my husband and I had to shop for some furniture for our new apartment. And I just felt so guilty all the while we were in the store."

"You felt guilty?" Puzzlement on my face.

"Yes. Father Robert emphasizes the evils of consumerism in a world that's filled with poverty. Of course, we felt guilty... off on a buying spree."

"But you were getting married! And everyone needs furniture, Caroline."

I explained to this young woman that marriage was a sacrament that deserves celebration without being showy or ostentatious.

"We did keep the wedding simple. My mother wanted something more elaborate, but I convinced her how selfish that would be."

I shared with Caroline, that my daughter had also shopped to set-up her house in New Hampshire, a few years earlier when she was married. Caroline had met Leslie and Jeff and knew they were self-less people, doing important work in social justice. I spoke with Caroline about the holiness of creating a home, one where love and joy, not guilt, can flourish.

Preaching, a responsibility of mine, was a joy. At the Vineyard Community and in retreat houses, I had also had opportunities to preach. And I savored it.

In the spring, I was contacted by *NBC Nightly News* with an in-quiry to film me at MIT as the campus minister. Wonderful! I alerted my children and mother to watch the show. Fr. Robert was indifferent, as long as it was not filmed in any of the religious buildings. I assumed it would be about an increase in lay ministers or some of the faith projects I had done in a secular university. It wasn't. Evidently, you don't always rehearse an interview for live news programs. As I sat on a bench in front of the chapel with a microphone in my face, questions came rapid fire.

"Do you want to be a priest? Will women never be ordained? How does it feel to watch a man command the altar every Sunday?"

The three-minute segment seemed to last an hour. I don't even know what I said. When I called my mother to see if she had watched it, she said, "Are you sure it was you? It was so radical I thought you were Jane Fonda." The best lift was from a Jesuit I knew in Asia. He said he savored hearing me rattle on in Japanese.

At a copy shop the next morning, I handed the Easter bulletin to Muriel, a middle-aged woman behind the counter. She glanced over the front page then looked up at me. "I saw you on NBC! You're Virginia. I've also seen you on Sundays at Mass. But, I don't think I have ever seen your name on the bulletin?"

"Oh well. Maybe next time."

"I don't know why Father doesn't have it in regularly." She reached over and clutched my hands and shook them. You count, too! Don't forget that. We all count."

In the evening at home and in prayer, I kept seeing Muriel shake my hands and hearing her say that I counted, too. My heart softened with consolation; I sensed and received the laying on of hands that signify ordination. One word came to me that night as I turned to God.

Relinquishment.

Over and over it began to haunt my prayer and evoke memories. *A woman, unable to concelebrate Mass with my peers. A lay minister, prevented from speaking at the NCCB conference. Even as wife, who can't have her husband attend the same church, because Fr. Robert thinks George will distract me from doing my "chores" during coffee hour.*

At one time I thought relinquishment was what you gave up for Lent. Later I believed it was something that you would not do because it was a sin, such as using birth control. Soon after I considered it as carrying a cross of some kind, for example, living with an alcoholic father. Now I realized relinquishment could mean taking the road less traveled—being a layperson who is called to ministry.

Renunciation of the priesthood could not be where I was, for it was never mine to relinquish. To renounce is to declare something an anathema, to banish something forever from one's life. I did not renounce the priesthood; it renounced me. Or rather the Vatican renounced me, all women, and married men.

Relinquishment has its ultimate meaning in Jesus on the cross. In my prayer I reflected on Jesus' resurrecting. Jesus did not laud or glorify his resurrection. He did not bring out the wine for a celebration. Jesus' passion in his resurrection was tied to his followers. His passion was their witness and mission. We got it wrong if we say the Church has a mission. It is mission that has a Church. God has given a mission to the people to 'build my Church,' and people are the crucial element of the Church.

During my prayer in the following weeks, I began to falter. I struggled with it over and over. I hated this relinquishment. I confessed to Jesus that it pained me to see rewards coming to others, simply because they are male.

So what if stickers on my car window let all of Cambridge know that I had two coveted parking spaces—one at a prestigious university and one at an exalted theology school? So what if I've been published in a Catholic journal and directed retreats? Relinquishment meant that I would never hear a confession, baptize a baby, be the celebrant at a wedding, or stand at the altar and lift the host. *Why have I chosen the road less traveled? I must either flee from prayer or from ministry. But then I hear You say, "You didn't choose. I chose."*

Once a year the cardinal of the Boston archdiocese met with campus ministers from each university. I drove us to our meeting. During the ride, Fr. Robert cautioned me from mentioning that I had attended the papal Mass in Washington D.C. "Of course. He doesn't need to know that a layperson got front seats to the Holy Mass at the National Mall."

Fortunately, Cardinal Medeiros was kinder and more receptive to laypeople than Fr. Robert or Pope John Paul II. He had a gentle face and a trace of an Hispanic accent, having come from Brownsville, Texas. The conversation began with Cardinal Medeiros asking Fr. Robert to describe the kind of work he was doing.

"Of course, I am in charge of eucharistic liturgies, the office, and I deal with alumni and students. I make sure the students know the proper doctrine, including how sinful abortion and birth control are, and that they read the bishops' peace pastoral. "

"And you, Virginia?"

"I try to deepen the spiritual lives of the students and listen to their situations—missing home, fear of failing. I created a prayer book for Lent and took a group of students to the Museum of Fine Arts to contemplate the paintings of the crucifixion and the passion."

"That is excellent. You're very caring."

"Thank you, Cardinal Medeiros."

"Robert, keep in mind that you are working with young adults and forcing moral doctrine might discourage them from coming to church. And encourage more of these projects that Virginia did."

Outside Robert turned to the right as I turned to the left. I called to him, "The car is over here."

"I'll get back on my own," he snapped and continued walking away.

On the last day of classes in May, I received an envelope in the mail from the MIT Catholic chaplain's office. The letter from Robert told me that next year I would be happier some place else. Therefore, I would not be needed at MIT in the fall. *I've been fired.*

I let the letter drop to the floor. Put my face in my arms. *How can I tell George? He worked so hard for me to get my degree.*

I had no redress. Although on campus he referred to me as campus minister, my name wasn't in the official archdiocesan listing of campus ministry. *Only the word Staff.*

The head of MIT's women's administrative office was furious and went to the chaplain's building only to be told it was a church matter over which she had no control. By the end of the summer Fr. Robert was no longer at MIT or at his religious order's residence in Boston; he'd been replaced by another priest from his religious order. However, by the end of summer I also had a new position—at Weston Jesuit School of Theology, guiding lay students.

13

A MONTH ON MISSION: PART I

A workshop presentation to a parish in Massachusetts, the
NALM conference in Colorado, the meeting of theologians
in New York, and and an ordination in Minnesota,
Summer 1983

I sat down at the dining room table and contemplated June of 1983, all I saw on my calendar were zigzags across the country–a workshop in Winthrop, a reunion with bishops and the National Association of Lay Ministers conference in Denver, a meeting of theologians in New York, an ordination in Milwaukee, a retreat in Duluth, and the National Council on Catholic Bishops annual meeting in Collegeville.

George chimed in optimistically, "I'll bring a bottle of champagne to Logan Airport, smash it against the plane, and christen your trip "a Month on Mission!'" Enthusiasm from him transformed my haphazard schedule into a cross-country adventure, a journey with a spiritual purpose. If I don't sport a white collar around my neck or vestments cloaking my body, if I'm not allowed to bless babies or change bread and wine, why not hit the road?

St. Ignatius sent his novices miles away with only two deniers in their knapsacks to discover where they might meet the Spirit in unexpected places. I have more than two dollars, but that's not going to cover my mission. After a subsidy for attending the conference in Denver and a stipend for leading a retreat for women in Duluth, how did I intend to earn my keep for the rest of the trip? The challenge was not to lose sight of my soul, which thrust me forward as I embarked.

Workshop at a parish in Winthrop, a Boston suburb

"Virginia, umm, that is Mrs. Finn, or, err, should I say Ms. Finn... is leading a spiritual workshop for the bouncers." *The bouncers?* The priest introducing me had the figure of a bouncer himself. His midriff was so broad the buttons strained against his black jacket. "Excuse me, for the ushers. Or do we call them greeters? Tough to know these days who's who with all the changes in the Church."

The Archdiocese of Boston had invited me to lead parish workshops for lay ministers. Among this group were lectors, eucharistic servers, religious education teachers, and now "bouncers," aka ushers. I felt stung for the half dozen men who had just been introduced to me. But they were thrilled when I explained that the ministry of hospitality had a long Catholic tradition and that welcoming believers at the door helped to prepare parishioners to welcome God during the Mass. One gentleman, with cherry red cheeks and fluffy white hair, slipped me a business card as we dispersed. "If you ever want to buy a house in our town, I'll be sure to get you the deal of your life."

In diocese after diocese, the number of lay leaders was mushrooming—some with graduate-level preparation and compensation, many who served in voluntary ministry like the ushers. The time was ripe to gather together, assert our presence, and plan for the future. It was time to travel, and summer promised it.

The National Association of Lay Ministry Coordinators Conference, Denver

Early followers of Jesus traveled on foot, on camel, on donkey, but obviously, not on American Airlines. Those ancient disciples had ample time to digest a real supper and avoided the quandary of those of us who flew a thousand miles to Denver, ate fast food out of plastic containers, arrived late in the evening, and fell into bed in a standardized dorm room at a Catholic college.

In the morning we were sitting in rows before a stage podium where the bishop of Denver was wishing us well beneath a bright banner that proclaimed that the people he addressed were part of a national gathering of lay ministers and coordinators. Beside the lectern a lush display of plants with leaves veined in pink caught my eye. As the day progressed, I occasionally rested my gaze on the leaves and let my ears go deaf. Nomenclature reigned: how we are named, how we name ourselves, how to claim a name that earned respect.

A collarless Catholic clergyman delivered the first presentation. "Laypeople do not depend on me as I had been taught in the seminary," he announced. "There, I was instructed that the folks in the pews needed to be told how to plug in. 'They want to be told,' I learned. Not so, I discovered out in the trenches. The agenda of the laypeople is not my agenda. The Church is my agenda. Not the people in it."

He's off on the wrong foot.

From the back came a catcall. "Are you saying that the Church is *not* its people?"

"No, no. I'm saying the world is the agenda of the people, but the Church is the agenda of its priests."

Another shout came from the audience, "What do priests know about the world to tell us?"

The second speaker was a male lay leader; his eyes, squinting under a shock of thick brown hair, seemed to agree with the audience. "Like my parents before me, I was given answers as a child and told to obey them. But as a young adult, I found the answers I was given didn't fit my life experience."

Animated audience applause. The speaker smiled, lifted his shoulders into a confident stance, stopped squinting, and went on. A period of open discussion followed. Though not a slugfest, unanimity was in short supply.

"Is this conference for volunteers or paid lay ministers?" a woman shouted from the audience.

From a man in priestly garb leaning on a door we heard: "I'm sure your parish receives great benefit from your generosity. But one dynamic that must be out is the full-time volunteer. Lack of standards and lack of supervision in these cases is bad news. Some people act as if they, not the pastor, own the parish."

Another shout, "I thought the people owned the parish!"

Denver was a gala of give-and-take that I had never experienced before.

The free-for-all in the morning had been intoxicating, heady, and cathartic. Creative tension—the byword for the mood in Denver—had, by the end of the afternoon, sapped my energy. I dragged my body to my dorm room and dumped it on the bed. An hour later I woke up. The drapes had been closed on my late arrival the previous night. I walked to the windows, opened the drapes, and sat on a chair. In the distance, but not far enough away to be mere background, the Rockies stunned me. There was a glory in the mountains, a mingling of nature's power with the ambiguity of shaded tones. Peace fell over me, comforting, consoling.

In the morning I attended a workshop titled *Compensatory Issues*. After having been advised by the priest who hired me at MIT to be content with minimum wage, I wanted to orient my compass regarding compensation. Twenty of us crowded around a long table in the dining room and, almost immediately, I was told the direction where my compass must point by a fellow with an auburn beard and a baseball cap. "None of us full-timers should get paid more than $4,000 a year."

While I tried to divide that annual amount by fifty-two weeks, a woman down the table gave a whoop. "Four thousand! I'm Bonnie and I have three kids. How can I raise a family on that? You're a dreamer."

"I have no trouble on less than $4,000." Across from Bonnie a blush spread over the face of a nun. It was pointed out that she got free room, board, and health insurance. But Sister had the pluck to respond with practicalities. "Parishes will never be able to pay the labor costs of lay ministers after relying on what we women religious have given them through our vow of poverty."

Bonnie didn't shy away from that one. "Without dressing it up with formal vows, some of us are damn poor." She paused and yanked her graying hair into a fresh ponytail. "It's tough being a lay minister."

"That's how it should be!" A cheerful voice was matched by a buoyant smile on a young male who looked as if he'd played hooky from a confirmation class. "If we minister, we're called to show that pastors live by gospel values."

"But they won't," came a quiet voice. "My husband and I minister in the same parish. We get paid so poorly that, at the end of the month, the priests let us take food that the parishioners have donated for soup kitchens. And, it doesn't make the priests humble. They joke about it."

The fellow with the auburn beard lifted his baseball cap to her. "Bless you, Betty! You and your husband are living gospel values."

"But our kids really resent it." Betty was close to tears. "Do we really have the right to impose poverty on our children?"

"There are no easy answers." Our facilitator's modulated voice repeated this three times during the session. "There are no easy answers, but there is a need to voice how we feel and where we are in the ministerial scheme of the Church."

We know that the ministerial scheme of the Church matters, as much as just pay, which would give respect and visibility to lay ministers as religious leaders.

That afternoon I let my eyes rest on the graceful pink veins of the leaves on the plants near the podium while the question of lay ministers' identities got a different going over. After the presentation, I heard voices but didn't bother to search for faces to match them. The initial suggestion was that we stop naming ourselves "lay ministers" and use our specialties to let people know who we were as ministerial leaders. "Lay ministry keeps us linked to the ordinary folks."

"I'm a director of religious education. It has dignity."

"I suppose I'm a religious educator, but I'm known as a catechist."

"Then you're not a DRE like I am? You just teach."

Class warfare every time a mouth opens? Responses bounced back and forth. I kept my eyes on the leaves.

Campus minister. Grief counselor. Pastoral associate. I used to be a nurse but now I'm a hospital chaplain. Youth minister.

I felt my mind drifting. *Here we are, raw recruits simultaneously trying to devise strategy for winning a war while nursing the blisters on our heels.* Neither the people in the pews nor their pastors would ever see us as other than the foot soldiers in the army of the Church. If they bothered to look at us at all.

That night sleep was my enemy. The more I wrestled to capture it, the more it fled from my grasp. I yearned to contemplate the mountains, not the curtain of darkness beyond my window, yearned to throw off the cloak of churchliness, yearned to be on my way to New York where George would meet me and embrace me.

Culminating in a fiery finale, a Western-style barbeque was held indoors in the dining hall where someone had hung a huge sign: THE PEOPLE'S REFECTORY. Who, in our band of rebels from Montana and Mobile, California and Cleveland, who in this microcosm of ministry in America, still had the energy to be that creative? Earlier we had stomped our infantry feet. We foot soldiers who were hardly recognized by the hierarchical Church had belted out "When the Saints Go Marching In." In New England, we seldom stomp or form rumba lines. We may holler to heaven but only at Red Sox and Celtics games. Certainly not at a religious gathering. *Am I a Puritan?*

I had smiled, laughed, and chatted aimlessly and amicably during the endless songfest initiated by The Singing Catholic Family of the Southwest. In the solitude and darkness of my dorm room, I saw the fecund family on the makeshift stage. The mother, my age, motherhood her habit. The father, barrel-chested and balding, led the songs, ones we had loved in the 50s and 60s. Behind him were four sons and a daughter. Beside the stage were the wives of the sons, babies in their arms.

The parents had been in lay ministry for twenty years! That news startled those of us who thought of lay ministry as a five-year-old invention. The family journey had been one struggle after another, the Father proclaimed. "Been thrown out of more parishes in the Southwest than you can count on a calculator!"

Then came "Puff, the Magic Dragon." They sang it with admirable harmony. Envy tinged my heart. Respect followed for their courage to initiate ministry while raising a large family. A simple sentence sparked the storm at sea within me. The sons and the daughter had followed their parents and become lay ministers. Hearing that, I felt a nearby mountain press down on me. I fled.

Was this disheveled folk-singing family the new model for Catholic ministry? Instantly I chided myself for my snobbish, New England put-down, just as "They wash not their hands" was leveled at the first disciples by the Pharisees. I was no better than the priest who put down the ushers. Or did my anguish come from challenges to my own identity as well as from my outrage as a mother? *How can parents do this?* They were like mothers in the old days who insisted that one son becomes a priest. Dissolving before my eyes, I saw the freedom each offspring deserved.

The revelation of this conference: *I am not into revolution.* I still cherished diversity in ecclesial identities—bishops, priests, brothers, sisters, and lay ministers. And the diversity of its people.

Playing Pick-Up Sticks was all we had done there, with identities and issues up for grabs. Prophetically riding the crest of the future had instilled a calling within me; but seeing the shoals of the future that week had sobered me up. The questions asked, the challenges thrown, the arguments and divisiveness. Serious questions emerged. Questions that had to be answered.

Who will do it? If lay ministers don't initiate the process, who will? *But it's so much easier to let others name you.*

A hornet's nest. Each challenge raised a sting on my skin, my soul. *Perhaps I sit in judgment of others because my own identity lacks clarity, not only in the Church, but also before God. How much is my naming myself a "ministerial female leader" God's anointing?*

Without ordination I feel like a mother out of wedlock.

And God? God was beyond me. Out of reach. As strong and silent as the majestic mountains.

Annual Catholic Theological Society, New York City

In New York City the heat of the street slapped my face as I left the bus from the airport. Steam blew high from manholes toward the sun. The "anything goes" spirit of Manhattan lifted my mood. Queue up again in the hotel. In spite of two desk clerks, the line for each equaled the beads in a decade of the rosary. In the elevator, on my way to the keynote presentation, panic momentarily prevailed as I noticed others wearing badges with Ph.D. before their name. *Stop. I belong here. I was invited by Fr. Dave, a board member! I'm a searcher, sifting through the human experience for God's immanence and transcendence.*

"Tell that to a keynote theologian," I murmured thirty minutes into his talk. God had not yet been mentioned, instead "vectors," a popular new term, appeared to substitute for the divine. "Paradigming" was another favored word.

After dinner, many of the other speakers and attendees met in a spacious and attractive suite for drinks and conversation. I helped put out the snacks. There were mostly priests, some in clerical garb, most in dark suits. The few women theologians, most of them nuns, wore dresses, subdued but attractive.

I was in my green blazer, bright scarf, and gold earrings that George had bought for me just for the trip. I was feeling slightly the outsider until I noticed in an alcove, a circle of chairs from which smoke was floating. I wandered over and asked if anyone had a cigarette.

As a fellow gave me one, he noticed my name badge. "Virginia Finn. Aha! The expert on celibacy. Please, please, join us." He motioned to where he'd been sitting. "Let me freshen your drink." He took the glass from me and walked into the room with the bar.

I noticed that in this area it was mostly men, casually dressed, with their jackets off, ties loosened, and shirtsleeves rolled up. "That was Phil, getting your drink. I'm Kevin," a man said extending his arm for a handshake. "I put your article that was in *Studies in the Spirituality of Jesuits* on my class reading list. So share your wisdom about celibacy."

Are you priests, ex-priests, laymen?

Kevin raised his eyebrows. "Well, speak up."

"I can't believe how many reading lists I've been on, but some have criticized my article for being too 'exact' in proscriptions."

"Ignore that! It was theology developed by the interface between the values of the Christian community and sexual reality."

Phil returned. "Now, Virginia. Ordination. Do you want it?"

"Yes. But I also really want the people in the pews to get involved with ministry. Are you all ordained?"

Phil said, "The collar's been round my neck for years."

"I was," Kevin murmured, pointing to a lovely young woman on the other side of the room. "We met at seminary together, and then we left together."

"Time out! We've finished the resolution and you're about to hear it," proclaimed a papal voice from the other side of the alcove.

Obedience was instantaneous.

The following day, Stephen read the petition he planned to bring before the full body of the theological society—to resolve to ensure peace on earth. My mind tried to fish out its main intentions, which seemed not only to support the peace march but also to condemn nuclear weapons, the arms race, and a continuance of military activism. Details to buttress each principle were there but fell from my radar screen.

With his last words, swords were drawn.

"It's long enough to be a dissertation!" Phil shouted.

"You know what that means," Kevin shot back. "Relegated to a committee and buried for the next five years."

"We got to get these guys to put their asses out in the street and march on Sunday!"

Everyone left the suite, exhilarated. I was excited and hopeful because George was supposed to arrive any minute. When I opened the door to my room, there he was, lying across the bed. He had his shirt off and a very suggestive look in his brown eyes.

"At last!" I proclaimed.

The next day, surrounded by placards, George and I let exhilaration surge through us, as we marched along the route of the peace march.

"BAN THE BOMB!"

"BAN THE BOMB!"

"BAN THE BOMB!"

Tierney, who was attending New York University, met us in front of the United Nations building. Unlike a militaristic march, it was a razzle-dazzle affair. A tuba player was near us, five trumpeters were ahead of him, and he was accompanied by a jester ringing bells with his hands and shaking his bell costume, which was as bright blue as the sky above the skyscraper canyons.

Tierney stopped. I bumped into her. She was looking at a giant mother figure. The swaying, tall puppet mesmerized us as it passed. A woman next to us told us that it was one of the creations by a peace community in the Northeast Kingdom of Vermont.

As the twenty-foot, black-clad mother bowed and bobbed, Tierney whispered, "She isn't beautiful, but you feel her embracing you."

I remember a colleague urging me to have "Jesus be my companion on my month on mission." Now I imagined Jesus in a conductor's hat going up and down the aisles, not collecting tickets, but collecting stories. Each person he encountered felt a sudden flush of freedom to name whatever was inside that troubled the heart, imprisoned the body or the soul—a withered spirit, leprosy, a hemorrhage of blood. Each person healed into acceptance of self, acceptance by society.

The stories in Scripture surprise, startle, scandalize. *Why do Church cultures dehydrate the Good News?* Without the peace faction, the theological convention seemed dry, held back by the risks of creativity. The most evocative theology in New York was in the streets. *But, maybe this disheveled lay ministry conference can eventually evoke some creativity.*

Ordination, Milwaukee

Lucky to find a seat on Amtrak's Lakeshore Limited, which was mobbed, I knew the entire night would be spent sitting up, my least favorite posture for sleeping. I fled to the lounge, also packed tightly but not so crowded to deny me and my two hot dogs a seat. As I ate I listened and realized that everyone was talking war and peace. Many had marched in the peace demonstration, their placards–Ban The Bomb–were tipped against the windows and hid the view, but even those who hadn't marched seemed engaged in conversation with those who had.

In the morning the sun, a blushing pink satin pillow, sat on the flat Indiana horizon. I instantly yearned to be back in the Manhattan hotel with George. Instead, I opened my eyes to my companions who were stirring, standing, stretching, smiling at one another. I closed my eyes again and hugged my body, knowing that in my heart there were no dropped stitches, no unraveled edges.

"You're up and about early." I said to the woman from Iowa who shared a lounge seat with me last night and who now offered coffee and a donut while I fumbled in my purse for money to pay her.

"Hey, it cost next to nothing. You enjoy it."

She was off to her own seat.

Perhaps because I was not fully awake, I heard in my head Jesus say, "I'd be at home riding the rails."

I nodded and grinned, remembering Father Phil at the CTSA conference telling me to have Jesus be my companion on my month on mission. I imagined Jesus in a conductor's hat going up and down the aisles, not collecting tickets, collecting stories. Each person encountered feeling a sudden flush of freedom to name whatever was inside that troubled the heart, imprisoned the body or the soul. Each person healed into wholeness, acceptance of self, acceptance by society.

The stories in scripture surprise, startle, scandalize. Why do Church cultures dehydrate the Good News of its revelatory dramatic power? Without the peace faction, the theological convention seemed dry, with little profundity, the talks peculiarly unfinished as if the vise of vows and Vatican surveillance held back the risks necessary for creativity. The most evocative theology in New York was in the streets. No doubt about that.

Also no doubt that right here on the train there were some great people who had made heroic efforts to get themselves to the Peace March. I might not have gone if I hadn't been thirty stories up in the Manhattan hotel and if theologians passionate about peace hadn't urged me to attend.

As the train approached Chicago, a question surged up like the skyscrapers emerging on the horizon, what is my mission for this month on mission? I'm a seeker. I'm yearning for God, someone seldom pinned down. What a flamboyant idea, pinning down God!

Being a searcher is a worthy vocation. As I own seeking my mission, tension dissolves. Discernment is another worthy vocation. Voyages promise situations calling for discernment. I grabbed that as another mission, though it seemed lame.

In Chicago I sat on a bench to wait for the train to Milwaukee. Union Station's mood and atmosphere seeped into me five minutes after departing from the Lakeshore Limited. Anyone who knows me well knows I hate being in limbo. But it wasn't the station that had me in limbo, it was my destination. I was headed to the ordination of Jesuits who would be installed in the priesthood; where I can only sit in the pews and watch. Beside me would be young women who would also not be installed; who would bow and genuflect to bishops, to priests, and to the seminarians about to become Alter Christus.

Men and women not in the ordained state–a third world country in Church geography– are housed in pews beneath that privileged niche of Sanctuary and Altar.

Hard to hang onto hope, let alone try to develop it within women ministerial students, whenever the confrontation is the Church's triumphal power. This time in a Milwaukee cathedral. Who will believe, during that ornate ritual, that the one thing to be valued is the vibrantly holy experience that installs us into the Kingdom that is God's own?

Wisconsin is New England stretched out like cling wrap with spacious miles between farms. The young boy in the adjoining seat shouts excitedly at the sight of chickens in front yards. He's from Chicago and has never visited Wisconsin. Over the Fleet Farm Mall in Germantown, he spots a blimp, claps his hands, and cheers my spirit.

Moving into Milwaukee the train stalls and I lose sight of him. Standing in the aisle for the wait, I watch a girl trying to become a woman as she tells her train acquaintance about an interview she had in Chicago for a job as a model for commercials. Her smoky eyes, long thick lashes and perfect brows are arresting and spell promise for her dream. Between us is a couple; a pretty girl who looks too wholesome to be in any commercial besides one selling Wisconsin butter. She talks and he's engrossed, bending toward her like Sir Lancelot, ready to pledge fealty. Finally, the train squeals, then lurches to a stop inside the station.

Eyes beaming, smile beaming, Peggy is waiting just off the platform with a bouquet of flowers. Her tan face, brown eyes, and brunette hair, framed by a soft, light yellow scarf around her head and neck, reminds me of a sunflower. One of the most affectionate women I've had the gift to know, she hugs me and puts her arm through mine to let me know, as we leave the station, that, though the ordination will be the most heart-wrenching stop on my map for the month, tonight we will try to forget tomorrow.

We're off to see a museum, she informs me once we're inside her ten year-old Honda. "Play tourist, Virginia, even if your stay with us seems only as long as the blink of an eye. You can't come to Milwaukee and leave thinking it's only breweries and Jesu."

"What's Jesu?"

"The Jesuit church near Marquette." Her words tumbled out with the speed of the accelerator on the car. "Did you think they're being ordained at the Cathedral? Wait till you see Jesu. It's unbelievably handsome, like one of the Jesuits being ordained. Marquette is a Jesuit university."

"Yes, I know. But what I don't know is whether I got an invitation to the ordination. I just took it for granted–"

"As well you should! You're an important part of the place where we're being formed for ministry. And we're going to the buffet reception afterwards." She swung into the entrance to a museum. "Ready for a little gossip? At the ordination in San Francisco, the parents weren't invited to the reception after the ceremony in church! The Jesuits took the recently ordained to a cleric-only party at a hotel. Some of the families had paid to cross the country and put themselves up. I'll tell you, it caused a b-i-i-g stink! No way are we intending to repeat that gaffe."

My heart skipped a beat. "What do you mean 'we'?"

"Those of us planning the ordination here in Milwaukee. I'm sort of included." She waved toward the building before us. "Here it is, the beauty queen of Milwaukee on our Great Lake!"

The setting of the museum by the water was unique. Wherever we were inside, whatever painting we contemplated, the lake was the frame. What other art museum had been so creatively utilized, Peggy bragged, and I believed her. In memory I knew the lake would pre-dominate over all the objects I was seeing inside the stark, white show-case. It was as if my eyes oscillated between an exceptional rose and a prize-winning lily, in the same vase.

Two hours later, in a German restaurant, I stared at fat bratwurst and fragrant sauerkraut, savoring them as much as the museum and its offerings. Peggy was telling me about her participation on the com-mittee planning worship at Jesu. She knew I was uncomfortable with her intention, after graduation, to work in liturgy. She would be ar-ranging for the many Sunday Masses; placing readers at the lectern without ever being able to preach from it, only because she was a wom-an. All in all, situations ripe for victimization. Bluntly, I broke into her conversation.

"Tell me about your ministry."

"That's what I'm doing, Virginia."

"No, you were telling me about your voluntary service planning worship. I want to hear about your Clinical Pastoral Education pro-gram at the hospital. Your supervised, professional ministry."

"Oh, my CPE." she groaned. "Well, being a hospital chaplain is an uphill climb if there ever was one."

"What ward do you have? Cardiac? Maternity?"

"The Emergency Ward! I can hardly believe it myself. Day after day, night after night, the ambulance brings people in with gunshot wounds, with attempts at suicide, with trauma wounds from horrible auto accidents." She grabbed my hand. "But I love it!"

"I could never do it, Peggy. Where I shined in my CPE program was with stroke victims, the quietist ward in the hospital. The only–"

"The ER is never quiet! Blood and guts. I deal a lot with family members. Just the other night…well, I did something you're not supposed to do." Her eyes darkened. "I certainly won't write up a verbatim for my supervisor on that one."

"What happened?"

"This man in his fifties. I can see him in his plaid shirt and chinos standing against a wall. When I went over to him he told me he'd just heard his son had been killed driving while drunk. Then he bent his head and said over and over, ' It's my fault. My sins were so bad, God took my son to punish me. God must hate me, so he killed my son to punish me.' He looked up then, into my eyes. And I just reacted. With both my hands I pushed his shoulders against the wall and said in a steady voice, 'No! No! No! God doesn't act like that. God doesn't punish by taking your son because of your sins. God loves your son, and God is trying to love you'."

"Peggy, what you did was out of compassion. Too sacred to turn into a verbatim that might get picked over by a supervisor." Inside, annoyance and empathy churned. I sighed. "That's one tough ministry you're doing."

"Exhausting, too."

"Then let's be on our way to wherever I'm staying. You have Mary and Evelyn to settle in yet tonight."

In the car, in response to her questions about the theological society meeting in New York City, I told her about the rebel peace group and the demonstration march. "The 20th Century's prime theologian was never mentioned. There'd been no Peace March if Gandhi hadn't lived and proclaimed and sacrificed. Forget Rahner, Barth, von Balthasar, Tracy, Tillich. Gandhi was the great theologian of the 20th Century. Gandhi, another St. Paul, neither mentioned at the convention of the theological society. Look at all the lives that have been transformed by that Indian prophet!"

"But I should still study my Rahner when I return to Cambridge in the fall." Peggy laughed. "Unfortunately, Gandhi wasn't a Jesuit."

That night I had the third-floor apartment all to myself. Peggy explained that her friend was visiting the Twin Cities over night and was pleased the apartment would have an occupant. The place was feminine but not a bit frilly, cozy in a way that said welcome. Peggy put the flowers in a vase, added water, and then said she had to run along to meet the other Weston students. She kissed my cheek. "I'm still at sixes and sevens about whether to write a verbatim on the father who lost his son. I don't know if I just want to keep the encounter to myself or whether I'm afraid of the supervisor judging my being so outspoken...we're warned constantly about that."

"Was God there in the experience?" I embraced her shoulder.

"Yes, yes, yes. In the honesty the father shared with me. I believe he was wrong in his believing God blamed him, but he was gut-wrenching honest about it." She walked to the door then turned. "And God was there in the honesty of my reply, even if I overstepped–"

"You saw the unbearable agony of the man. You reached out in compassion." I took her chin in my hand. "Maybe you were a symbol of God for him. Peggy, can you sit with that idea for a while?"

She bit her lip. Her eyes teared up. "I'll try." She mumbled. "Pray for me tomorrow, Virginia." She opened the door. "The sitting on the sidelines of an ordination won't be easy."

As soon as she had left, I collapsed on the sofa and prayed for her. Most of the women students participate in worship, but make a wide circle around responsibilities for liturgical events. Too close, too painful, too frequent a reminder of the denial. But not Peggy. She was gifted in the talents needed for genuine and creative worship; but she was not commonsensical. For that I feared she would pay a steep price.

Before taking a shower, one I promised myself would be long and luxuriant, I dug out my phone credit card and called George. He had news. Sister Martha had called. "She sounded nunny. She went on about breaking her wrist, an accident and that time she had rationed to help you lead your retreat will be shortened. Why does she think you need help?"

"George, she broke her wrist, poor thing. Anyway you think all sisters are nunny. And I'm much too relaxed here to worry, I'm luxuriating in a three room apartment all to myself. For the whole night and all day tomorrow until–"

"The ordination. You still think you have to attend?"

"I dread it. But I have to be there for Peggy, Mary and Evelyn."

"Give 'em each a bear hug from me. Dammit I wish I could give you more than a hug."

"Then come on out! Take some vacation time and sign up for my retreat in Duluth."

"I'll pass. You're so busy, you won't really have time to spend with me!"

Midmorning I woke up and lolled. The sun streamed through the windows but did not jar my sleep. The ordination was downtown and late afternoon, place and time where it belonged. I was here and nothing would budge me from the solitude of the present. The bed was near the windows. When I nudged my body up on the pillows, I could see neighboring roof tops. Milwaukee's flats. Across the street was a pink house with a roof, outlined in white like trim on a pink blazer. Next to it, the roof was a nun's blue cowl.

Eventually I engineered the coffee maker in the kitchen but returned to the bedroom while it perked, fascinated by the door near the bed that went to a part of the roof, complete with summer furniture. Across the way sat a couple in chaise lounges on their roof. Owners of the bar on the first floor?

Not brave enough to venture onto the roof, I sipped my coffee in the kitchen and admired a floor to ceiling piece of macramé. Made by the owner whom I don't know. She collects miniature camels. Ones made of wood, of glass, of pottery. None made of plastic. I like them, and I like her though I doubt that I'll ever meet her in person. I've only met her through her place. And her generosity.

Around noon I made a sandwich and took it, with a tumbler of ice tea, onto the roof and sat in a wooden and canvas director's chair near a small table. No other roof had company so it seemed as if just me and the sky might be friends for lunch. In the distance were breweries, tall commercial buildings, and steeples, one of them Jesu, where in a couple of hours I'd be kneeling, sitting, standing. Politicians get elected, teachers gain experience and more degrees to become principals and superintendents, business people work their way up the ladder unless a relative owns the company. Crazy the way religious leaders are chosen, I sputtered to myself.

In my tradition, until now, they go off with only those of their own gender, promise to never participate in a sexual act, and vow to obey God's will which comes through a superior–a bishop, cardinal, pope or if, like the Jesuits, they belong to a religious order, a provincial. The Jesuits do it up big, above the provincial is the General. 'Father General' sounds like a contradiction in terms though the present one is a saint oppressed by a pope.

I nodded at the clouds. Yes, above the whole Society of Jesus she-bang the Holy Father trumps the Father General because the Pontiff is the Vicar of Christ.

Regardless of religion, I mused, ancient ways lead to a dualistic separation of leaders from people. The monastery, which at one time was a sacred central place for the people surrounding it as well as a sanctuary for those on escape, seems for some today to be a rabbit hole where men practice being mute to each other in order to talk to God. Its very eccentricity in today's world bestows symbolic power even if no monk, though the possibility is legitimate, becomes a pope.

Finishing my sandwich and my babbling to myself, I scanned the horizon again and saw a mosque where the call had gone out for Muslim believers to pray. I climbed back into the apartment, slammed my duffel bag on the bed, pulled out my navy dress, and set up the ironing board. Slapping the iron up and down over the white collar and on the navy fabric, I suddenly didn't give a damn if I scorched it. All of them, for ages and ages, were men! Men who kept dictating rules and preaching while they siphoned off to women all the duties that smacked of caretaking.

Why does leadership have to be tied to ordination? Carry the Virgin Mary through the streets in a festive procession but keep those of her gender like statuary in the church to which she's returned.

Jesu, the huge Jesuit church or seemingly huge by its well-lighted white walls with red trim, was partially filled with families and friends of the about to be ordained, when Mary, Evelyn, and I found an empty pew, to the side but near the front. The younger women put me between them. Each chatted nervously with me, Evelyn pointed out the contemporary baptismal font not far from the altar; Mary whispered that, for the ordination, one hundred singers made up the choir. Her wavy brown hair tickled my shoulders each time she turned toward me, Mary voiced her intention of holding off any negative reactions to the ceremony until later.

"For the next two hours I just want to savor the experience for the sake of the Weston guys getting ordained." The brown iris in Mary's eyes appeared intentionally purposeful.

Evelyn, running a hand through her cap of blonde hair, turned her face with its shinning pink cheeks toward me. "I'm not here for the men! I'm here so Peggy won't have to go through the whole damn thing alone. Why on earth did she agree to sing a solo?"

The organ prelude gave way to the opening hymn that the grandiose choir insured resonated throughout the church. None of us needed to sing. Instead we stood, turned and stared at the rear of the nave where priest upon priest upon priest glided down the aisle. Only in the Heartland, I say to myself, would the choice for vestments be red, white, and blue. New England is too close to Rome for a display of Americanism.

By the time the bishop was enthroned, the master of ceremonies, a priest we all knew, had lined up those to be ordained as well as the visiting priests—each assigned according to his ranking—seated beside the altar, the rest huddled into pews beside us.

Mary had changed her mind, "Cripes, I forgot there'd be a zillion clergy. I may not be able to wait till later to react. I can't even see the Weston ordinands."

Evelyn was already dabbing at her eyes with a tissue. "If I wasn't shy and didn't feel so claustrophobic, I would stand up, Virginia, and shout, 'I'm ready, willing, and able'!"

Slowly, one by one, the young Jesuits put their bodies face down on the carpeted center aisle to prostrate themselves in submission to God, the profoundly moving and symbolic part of the ordination liturgy, a segment of the ritual that my longing to be one with them was most intense.

Peggy's solo voice lifted the accompanying litany into the sanctuary and, as a blessing, over them humbling themselves. The heartbreak of it shattered what little composure I had been able to sustain. Tears came. I closed my eyes to cover them. But on the I the long bus ride to Duluth, I learned that I can't close my heart to the pain.

14

A MONTH ON MISSION: PART II

Retreat in Duluth and National Conference of Catholic Bishops Meeting in Collegeville, Minnesota, Summer 1983

The bus from Milwaukee to Duluth took five hours. Plenty of time, too much time, to reflect on the ordination. I remembered Evelyn's mantra–ready, willing and able.

These women *are* ready. I said to myself or to God or telepathically to the bishop. Those young women were even ready to embrace celibacy. These women were willing, even to kneel at the feet of the bishop, as their Jesuit companions from school had done, and promise obedience to the will of the Church's hierarchical leaders. These women were as able and as educated in scripture, sacraments, and theology as any man being ordained. They were more willing than most to grapple with some of the agonies of ministry, like Peggy does, day after day dealing with traumas and tragedies in an ER. *Ordain them!*

Duluth

Pausing on the stairs at the graceful, large, shingled retreat house, I realized I knew more about Milwaukee than the city where I was to reside for the week, Duluth. Sister Martha had met my bus. The bad news was that her broken wrist was still in a cast, but we made the drive in one piece. The good news was that several women had signed on for the retreat that I would be directing. My sigh of relief, not worthy of the disposition intended for my soul, was the dispensation of a stipend, one that might support most of the remainder of my mission month. At the retreat house, Sister Martha delivered me into the capable hands of Sister Margaret Mary.

Due to her advanced age and her long habit, Sr. Margaret Mary climbed stairs, crossed landings, and moved across the carpeted floors in slow contemplation, giving me time to savor the bedrooms I gazed into. Spacious windows in each were curtained in white organdy which billowed in the breeze and offered views of fruit trees in abundant flower. I sighed again, grateful that one of these rooms would be mine. "In which room shall I put my luggage, Sister?"

She turned to face me. Her eyes were mischievous. "Follow me."

We ascended steep, narrow stairs. Maybe, as the retreat leader, I would get a suite. As if reading my thoughts, Sister stopped on the top step and whispered over her shoulder, "The retreat mistress deserves the best."

She moved aside to make way for me. Into the attic. Due to the low roof, I bent my head which she mistook for reverence. "Ah, yes." Her palms came together in jubilation. "Here is our poustinia."

She mistook my groan for a murmur of appreciation. As she pointed to a pallet raised up on a wooden cot, I protested in silence, I've slept in trains, dorms, borrowed beds, but I'm here for a week. Could I please have a bed. I don't even want the organdy curtains.

"I will leave you now to your supplications for the graces of your retreat. If you don't wish to fast, supper will be served downstairs at six." She raised her eyes reverently, "Unless you want me to bring a tray to the poustinia."

I assured Sister that, not only would I descend for dinner, but also for a lovely walk around the lovely grounds in the lovely twilight. She left content.

On the following morning, Sr. Martha introduced me to my retreatants. At first glance any outsider might have assumed that the three women in plain skirts were nuns, and that a woman in a pastel pantsuit and another in a floral printed, tight fitting dress were laywomen. The reverse being true hardly surprised me; the cross-dressing struck me as a neon sign advertising Vatican II.

An elderly woman, short and stocky, entered the room from the direction of the chapel. She announced that a Mass would start in fifteen minutes. That ignited Sister Rosemary, in the floral dress, who dashed to the coffee maker and poured herself a cup. In an instant, Alice, the laywoman with a gray skirt, proclaimed for all to hear, "I can't have coffee! How can you have coffee with less than an hour before you receive communion?"

Turning to face them, Rosemary ran her hand impatiently through her dark curly hair before she shot back, "Time has nothing to do with food and communion these days! I hope this retreat doesn't mean being dragged back to the Middle Ages!"

Sister Gratia in the pantsuit added, "Who pays attention to all that legalistic malarkey anymore?"

"I do!" Marcelline, in a beige shirt, practically shouted. "Why don't we check with Father about this?"

"Why?" Rosemary calmly refilled her coffee cup.

Taking a slow, deep breath, I walked toward the windows and stared at the backyard. Beautifully terraced, it sloped toward a stream initiated by a small waterfall to the left of the house. Time to get everyone lost in the contemplation of nature.

We gathered again, in a circle, sitting on benches under a pear tree. "To collect ourselves," I began. "We will utilize, for the remainder of the morning, that incomparable monastic blessing–silence. You can start by taking a contemplative walk, alone, and discover the grounds. At lunch you can start to talk together. Contemplation will precede conversation."

"What exactly is contemplation?" Agnes asked. "How do I do it?" Agnes, in the blue skirt, earnest in her inquiry, had quizzical eyes that matched the blueness of her skirt.

"Really." Rosemary muttered.

"Agnes, I'm so glad you asked that question!"

"It's ok to talk now?" Agnes smoothed her skirt, put a hand in its pocket. She was younger than the other two laywomen.

"Well," I replied. "Questions for clarification of my directions are ok."

I hurried on, afraid of encouraging her too much. "Agnes, you start by leaving behind where you've come from–"

"Iron Mountain." Agnes frowned.

"Yes, well, you leave behind where you've come from to be where you are." I let my long arms drift. "Jesus, you know, was totally present to wherever he found himself…whether in a Samaritan village talking with a woman by a well or on a lonely mountain being in silence and solitude with God."

Agnes, having helped me launch the task, looked up with piety lighting her face. I moved further into their assignment of contemplation by urging that they really notice their surroundings; let themselves be drawn away from self through a blossom or branch, savoring what's been noticed, and then share it with God. Intently I shared what was Jesus' word–consider.

"Consider. Jesus said 'consider.' Glance at the lilies was not his message. He did not say, 'As you pass by, glimpse out of the corner of your eye those lilies in bloom.' Consider was the word spoken, the verb used. Stay right in that place beside the lilies. You might feel drawn to stroll among them, to take a deep breath and inhale their fragrance. To give gaze with love on them. To savor their beauty."

As they left, I paid no attention as Rosemary whispered, "But the lilies aren't in bloom yet." I was watching Agnes, who was already fixed upon a bud in the tree.

While they drifted away on what I hoped would be individual, personal perusal of nature, I headed for the house for a third cup of coffee, one that might help me reflect on how to help my five disparate retreatants for the next few days.

When gathered at lunch for our first open conversation, it was a task Gratia took up with gusto by announcing that she had marched in New York City for the peace demonstration against nuclear weapons. Not intending to burst her balloon, I shared that, while attending the Catholic Theological Association convention, I had also been a participant.

Rosemary took the reins then, inquiring about various theologians and famous scholars. Had I met them? Were women theologians included? What was the central topic?

Realizing our dialogue was unintentionally excluding the three laywomen from Iron Mountain territory, I excused myself and went into the kitchen where I thanked Sr. Margaret Mary for the delicious lunch and where I hoped my absence might coalesce the group. As I turned to rejoin it, I overheard talk about fishing. Fishing? Where do guys fish around here? Oh, yes, the Great Lakes. Eavesdropping more intently I discovered they fished, these women with very different backgrounds. Divisiveness was eased by a common sport.

For the afternoon, I gave another short presentation on intimacy with God, suggested the chapel for prayer, and invited them to join me later under the tree where we could come together in community to share our personal spiritual stories.

By four in the afternoon a cool breeze was drifting across the fields with the nodding tall grasses. The women appeared from different directions but with cardigan sweaters or crocheted shawls across their shoulders.

Rosemary was offering an apology and asking forgiveness from the laywomen for having been abrupt with them when they first met.

"Just a hint of the pre-Vatican II Church will do that to me. And your chiding me for having food or drink before communion was too much. But I am sorry. I offended you."

She opened her heart then to ask Alice, Marceline, and Agnes to try to understand the humiliations she had suffered before the changes of Vatican II.

The times when she had to crawl on her knees across the refectory floor to beg forgiveness from Mother Superior Luke for a small infringement of a rule like spilling a little food on the floor. "If I didn't manage to recite two rosaries and three litanies a day, I'd drown in guilt. All my soul had in it was shame," Rosemary paused, her voice choked up. "And fear. Fear of Mother Superior, fear of the bishop and the pope. Mostly fear of God."

"But you're not like that at all now. How did you get so strong and confident?" Agnes, voice alive with curiosity about a cloistered world, whispered her questions. "Did you change when you removed your habit? Or was it when you got a real job?"

Rosemary tossed her head back and laughed when a breeze rifled her curls. "There wasn't one particular thing that prompted it. Just one day, I decided to shave my legs. Then I put on shorts and knew I was free!'"

"What's your story, Alice?" I prompted.

"Tell them what you do, Alice," Marcelline urged..

"It's nothing. Just folks coming to our house several times a month. We pray together and share together. Some even bring some food to share."

"And you talk to us, Alice. You preach the gospel." Marcelline had a warm smile on her face.

The Sisters sat forward, their eyes intent on Alice

"Watch out, Marcelline! I don't exactly preach. And It's my turn to tell my story. You can tell your own."

"But you're on the diocesan–"

"Marcelline!" Alice shakes her finger in her friend's direction. She then continues, "Yeah, I'm on a diocesan team. Thank God for Bishop Anderson. Sometimes I stay as long as a week in a parish, if it's pretty far away. Then I have to take short courses to keep up with... my responsibilities."

"With your *ministry*," Rosemary interjects.

"Well, let's not get too carried away. No fancy business in Iron Mountain territory. I carry my office around with me in the car as well as my tape recorder and tapes. I can't sing worth a damn." Alice rubs her scrubbed, shiny forehead with a hand. "I'm sixty-one years old and

I dream and dream of all I've not yet done for the Lord. I feel He's calling me…That's it. Amen."

Gratia begins but I don't hear her. I'm lost in thought about the tremendous tenacity of Alice. The first Catholic Pioneer Woman I've known. Her tall sturdiness masks her interior humility, and I feel humbled by her. In one way she seems to place herself on the bottom rung of the Church ladder that is Church but she trusts God's call, senses it intensely.

Shaking my head in order to be with the others, I hear Gratia's voice. Reciting a litany. Promoting her causes. Feminism. Challenging Clericalism. Prison Reform for Women. Anti-war. Anti-nuclear Power. Empowering Native Americans. Moving Forward Civil Rights.

A bundle of issues is Gratia. We don't know who she is. Does she?

"Time is getting away from us." I break in. "We haven't heard Agnes."

"Not too much to say." Agnes is birdlike in her movements as she perches forward on her bench. "One of eleven children. The oldest so, of course, I never had time to play. I was the second mother, yet, when I was a child I had my own contemplative moments … like when it snowed … or I was in the forest with the tall trees."

"What is your spiritual desire, Agnes?" I ask.

"I don't know how spiritual it is, but I'd give anything to get away from Iron Mountain. I know it sounds too ambitious, but I'd really love a job in Duluth. But my Dad is sick and, as the oldest … well, y'know." Agnes has stolen my heart. All she wants is to get away from where she was born which was, long ago, all I wanted.

"And what do you do, Rosemary?" Agnes quickly asked, deflecting attention away from herself.

"I'm a hospital chaplain."

I've known many Rosemarys at Weston. What she doesn't like is being taken for granted by the priests. As she said, "Only they can bring communion to the patients. Only the priests can do the last rites... sacrament of the sick. It's heart-breaking when someone comes into the emergency room, is dying, and needs the last rites. Father is nowhere to be found. But I can't do the last rites the patient is begging for. Sickening."

"Let's have a prayer before you have dinner," I say.

"Hail Mary, full of grace..." Marcelline initiated.

After dinner we drifted toward the den where Sr. Margaret Mary had lit a fire and put out a pot of coffee. Five minutes by the fire seemed to loosen up Gratia.

"I'm not in New York City marching for peace now." She placed her coffee cup on an end table and clapped her hands. "But I still remember the graffiti in the Manhattan subway station. That was a revelation to me!" St. Gratia threw her head back in laughter that infected us all.

We were quiet for long minutes. Then it was Gratia who spoke again. "I haven't really leveled with you. Do you want me to?"

Nods moved faces but no one spoke.

Gratia sat up but as spoke she stared into the fire. "As soon as I get back, I'll be meeting with my AA group. I even went to one in New York City... Met some tough birds at that one."

"How long have you been going?" Alice asked.

"Five years. I was kind of a wreck. Sister Wreck I called myself before I got sent to a Guest House five years ago."

I swallowed the lump in my throat. *Did they have those when my father was still alive?*

"You're no longer a wreck," Rosemary whispered. "You're Gratia who happens to be a woman religious."

"My husband goes to AA. Up in the Iron Range," Marcelline confessed. "It's good for him so it's good for me."

"I've never been to the Iron Range," Rosemary said. "Tell us about it. Virginia seems to travel everywhere. But you haven't been there, have you?"

"No, no. I'd like you to tell us about it."

"Phooey!" Agnes exclaims.

"But they should know about it." Alice's face is determined.

"So what is it, the Iron Range? All I know is that it's north of –"

"The Iron Range was the largest pit iron mining range in the world," Alice adds. "When I was a girl all the mines were open. Well, they were so deep into the earth that if you stood on the edge and looked down, the bulldozers looked like toy trucks."

"But now most of them are closed. You know what that means?" Marcelline said, "That means about 60% unemployment."

"Sixty percent? I've never heard of much more than 6%" I said.

"You know what sixty percent means?" Marcelline continued, knowing that Rosemary, Gratia and I didn't know. "It means crummy dilapidated houses in towns filled with misery."

"Some of the Indians have work," Agnes broke in. "The Jibway and Chippewa, they harvest wild rice. In all the world, Indians are the only ones with permission to harvest wild rice."

"It's not that easy a job." Alice went on. "Two men in a canoe go into kind of a swamp and hit the rice with paddles to collect it."

"Our whole region is polluted from the iron mines."

"Yes." Agnes added. "The landscape looks raped."

"That's not the only kind of rape," winced Alice.

"What are you talking about, Alice?" Rosemary bent forward.

"Don't Alice," Agnes demanded. Where did this Agnes come from?

Alice opened her arms in a gesture of futility. "I'm talkin' about the fathers– just some of them, especially when they're drunk. They take their teenage daughters, the ones who are virgins, and have sex with them, so they'll know what to do on their wedding night. That's their excuse."

"Pigs!" Gratia stared into the fire.

Agnes, in a heated voice, exclaimed, "My father never did that! We're a good Catholic family." Then her words petered out. "But two of my friends–"

Alice put her arm around Agnes. "No, no. Most of the Catholics don't–"

"Sometimes it's cousins. No one talks about it, but everyone knows it's happening," added Marcelline.

She was interrupted by Rosemary who grasped the laywoman's hand. "That's sickening." Rosemary's face had become as red as the flames.

"You have so much to put up with where you live. And, Alice, you're ministry must be agonizing, much more than mine."

Alice's eyes filled. She nodded over and over.

Before the evening ended a salt-of-the-earth unity collected us six into a close bond. Rosemary had promised to come to the Iron Range and attend Alice's next gathering for prayer in her home.

After checking with Sr. Margaret Mary about arrangements for the following day, our last day together, I climbed the stairs to my poustinia. My hard pallet got a welcome from me. The sufferings shared by the laywomen had driven away any desire left for a room with organdy curtains.

Tonight we listened to each other's word for the heart in it. No longer was I the retreat mistress. The centerpiece of our being together was the animated, compassionate dialogue among all of us, not between me and the others, not between the nuns and the laywomen.

Intensity about the Church had lessened in proportion to intimacy among women forming a small but vibrant community, submerged in the more visible Church.

Late the next afternoon we gathered under the tree for a final prayer service in which each retreatant offered a heartfelt prayer. To sum up, I closed my eyes and reminded them of how Jesus contemplated real lives, reached out to suffering lives, and revealed images of God that came from ordinary life. "He paid attention to what he saw around himself, let himself be absorbed in the particular, yet never let it impede his destiny. You have been contemplative in our time at this blessed place; let that move you forward more deeply into your destiny."

"Oh-h-h."

I opened my eyes and glanced to the side where Agnes, sitting on the grass, was writing on a pad. "What are you doing, Agnes?" I whispered.

She held her pencil in a dainty gesture. "I didn't catch the last line of your prayer."

Sorrow flowed into my heart. "You, Agnes, must trust the beauty of your own relationship with God. There's no need to borrow another's."

Then they're gone. These women who are everywhere. Without them there would be no Church. They are the buttress that keeps the Church standing.

Collegeville

My next jaunt was to Collegeville, a three hour drive from Duluth. Fortunately, I shared it with another lay adviser, Donna. She and I had planned on going only for the day, and would drive back to Duluth after dinner. Collegeville, the site of the National Conference of

Catholic Bishops annual summer gathering, was also where we would meet with Bishop Paul Anderson and others who had served with us on the last NCCB Laity Committee. The site was operated by the Benedictines, and comprised of a college, a conference center, and a church the size of a cathedral. When the church came into view on the highway, it struck me as a giant futuristic animal.

Sadly, the bishops standing outside as we arrived looked as traditional as ever. In contrast the soft folds on the face of Bishop Paul lifted my heart.

He grabbed a hand of each of us. "But I've made a terrible mistake. I hope you'll forgive me." Donna and I waited, in silence.

"The conference isn't finished! It ends tomorrow. How could I have gotten so muddled? You have to stay overnight so you can participate tomorrow in the last Mass of the conference."

I rattled on about that impossibility—I didn't bring my toothbrush and my luggage was back in Duluth. But Donna only asked, "Where do we stay?"

"Where will you stay? Right here with us in the residence."

"With all these bishops!"

"'Of course. They're harmless, most of them. We've got empty rooms. Even a Cardinal's."

Is Bishop Paul out of his mind? A woman, a laywoman, stay in a Cardinal's room? I saw the headlines in The Boston Globe, 'Feminist Steals Cardinal's Bedroom.'

"Bishop Paul, isn't this unorthodox?" I was relieved that at least he hadn't suggested I stay in the Cardinal's room.

"Well, yes. But don't worry, Virginia." He reached out to pat my arm. "Now here's some money." He thrust bills into Dona's hand. "Drive into town, get what you need for an overnight, have a fancy dinner, and meet me back here around nine. That sounds about right."

After our excursion into town, a contingent awaited us with re-freshments in the conference center lounge. They were all bishops who had served, as we had, on the committee established by the body of bishops to activate and inspire laypeople.

After welcoming us, the bishops began asking about what they called my "pilgrimage." Each was amazed that I'd embarked alone on my month on mission. I needed little prodding to advertise the vibrancy of the gathering of lay ministers in Denver, the peace activism among theologians in Manhattan, and the agony of the ordination in Milwaukee. My summer spiritual journey, I was told while I sipped a gin and tonic, was more captivating than the bishops' pilgrimage to Collegeville.

Bishop Paul must have noticed that Donna was beginning to tire after our three-hour drive. He jumped up, voiced profuse apologies again for being remiss, and directed us to our rooms. Mine was a suite, complete with a fruit basket, cheese and crackers, and a bottle of wine on the table. Bishops are treated royally. *Maybe I should petition God to consecrate me a bishop. Petitioning the pope would be useless.*

Hurrying into the new nightgown bought in town, I shut off the light and slipped under the sheet and blanket in the side room where the bed was.

Like the bishop who was scheduled to be in this room, sleep was a no-show. The room was broiling. My head was spinning. I pulled just my shoulders up to the windowsill. Took deep breaths of air. Watched black pants walk past. Saw other black-clad bishops go by.

My eyes continued to spy. The breeze was calming. I rested my elbows on the sill. *Why am I here?* I contemplated these rulers of the American Church. My eyes glued themselves onto the red bindings of a man walking toward my window. The red band and trim told me he was a cardinal. Instantly I crouched down and raced to the other room. Found the fruit basket. Removed the wine bottle. Opened it. Took a swig. Unwrapping a packet of crackers, I shoved one in my mouth. Nibbled another as if I were a mouse escaping from a cat. The crackers made my mouth dry. I took another swig of wine.

Sunshine and happy spirits woke me in the morning in time for Mass. My body and heart dithered with freshness and vitality as I entered the mammoth church. Within its dim interior, I found a pew, not too far front, not too far back. Bishops entered. Soon I was surrounded by them, though a few gathered around the altar. *I am the only woman here.*

My heart hummed. *But, I am here. Standing in place of all the women in the church. Alice. Marceline and Agnes. Sisters Rosemary and Gratia. All the women preparing to be ministerial leaders. The women theologians and the laywomen in Denver.* As the liturgy moved forward, I heard none of it. Instead, I heard the names of women from my past—my mother who had forty-two jobs, most of them in mills, and my French grandmother, a mother of ten sons and three daughters, who never spoke a word of English. The many women across our country and in our Catholic history who do not have a vibrant sense of God's consolation, because they believe that God cannot be within them, unless there is the mediation of a priest.

"You'll Never Walk Alone." As I walked to receive Communion, within me I heard the song and asked God to savor the people who are faithful so we never walk alone.

While we were at worship, Donna had saved a table for our committee bishops and me. Episcopal leaders, one after the other, stopped by to be introduced. On the one hand, I was the lovely lady who had shared Eucharist with them; on the other, they wanted to know just who this intruder was. Soon, we were shoving luggage into automobile trunks for the long trek north. There was Bishop Albert, towering over me; Bishop Jim, as comfortable in a straw farmer's hat as with a miter; and Bishop Ray, too liberal to be advanced out of his huge rural diocese. I was to go with Jim and Albert after a stop at the hospital to visit Cardinal Medeiros and bring him a gift. He became sick shortly after he had arrived and had missed the conference.

Reunion at Bishop Paul's Residency, Duluth

By late afternoon we were back in Duluth. By early evening, the bishops in mufti, were watching Bishop Paul waving barbeque implements and sporting an apron with the picture of a huge lobster on it. "Just to please our New Englanders. But we have only trout and venison."

At the picnic tables, which included personal friends of the bishop, a former mayor, a city council woman, a doctor, and a grocer, stories of fishing and hunting expeditions held sway. The councilor asked if I'd ever had elk lasagna. "It's unbelievably delicious," she stated.

The next morning, the banter over breakfast made my fingers fumble. Never could I live in community! George and I hardly talk at breakfast, which is a contemplative time for each of us; we watch birds through the window in companionable silence. Here it was chatter, chatter, chatter.

Bishop Paul invited his brother bishops to visit some of his parishes. They all enthusiastically assured Paul that there was nothing they'd rather do. "And you, Virginia?" Bishop Paul wiped strawberry jam from his chin.

"I'll stay here and rest." *Church, church, church. Don't they tire of it?* I spent the morning by a waterfall, praying in gratitude for my mission month. I felt peace with myself and with God. Although I was as far north as my mission intended to take me, my heart had already embarked on the road home. Bishop Paul would be taking me to St. Paul where I'd get the train to go east.

By now I'd imagined that I'd become acclimated to the vulnerability of being a lone traveler, dependent on a host's timetable and idiosyncrasies. At the start in Denver at the lay ministry conference, I'd been defensive and judgmental. Accepting vulnerability had been hard earned through the rest of the journey. Erasure of expectations and desires was the ascetical dimension of a mission trip.

When the bishops returned from their tours, it was affectionate good-byes as they left to return to their home dioceses. Jim said I was welcome to stop by in Toledo. Bishop Paul urged me to hurry. "I've got to be in the Twin Cities by dinner time. Run upstairs and get your suitcases. We've got to go now!"

We were leaving Duluth in a flurry. But as soon as we were in the car, Bishop Paul let me know that he looked forward to this drive in order to have a serious talk with me.

"Can I tell you about the decision I'm making?" he asked.

"Of course. What's the matter?"

"Nothing's the matter. I'll be seventy on my birthday. Yep. The ripe old age of seventy." He glanced at me. "And I think I'll resign. What do you think?"

I stupidly blurted out, "Are you going to get married?"

He laughed. "Married? What on earth put that idea in your head?"

"Almost every priest I've known, or heard about, left to get married." I was puzzled. "Can bishops resign? Just like that? I've never heard of a bishop resigning early. They can't get laicized, can they?"

"Me, reduced to the lay state? My goodness, you're dramatic." He was smiling again. "All I want to do is resign as ordinary of the Diocese of Duluth."

"I don't think you can do that." My voice was flat, at a loss on how to put it delicately. "Being in charge is too much for you? You're ill?"

"No, no, no. Bishops can offer their resignations to the pope at age seventy-five. I'm considering it at seventy. Stop playing high chief of a diocese."

"But why?"

"Because too many of us old duffers hang on too long!" Bishop Paul's voice had a fierceness that I'd never heard from him before. "Maybe I'll set an example by resigning. Give up the reins of power that can corrupt. Don't hang on! Let go!"

"But what will you do?"

"Become an auxiliary bishop again. Revert back to junior status."

"In Duluth?"

"No, no, no. To be the emeritus in Duluth wouldn't work." He rubbed his chin. "I know folks who will be thrilled to be rid of me. They'll want to put in an organization man."

"Well, thank you for letting me know ahead of time."

He stopped at a traffic light. Signs told me that we were nearing Minneapolis. He turned to face me. "I'm not letting you know. I'm asking your advice, Virginia. What do you think? My heart tells me that my desire is to do spiritual direction with parish priests. Help them connect with God. There's a bishop friend who'd be glad to have another auxiliary. What do you think?"

"Give me a minute to digest it." I turned my head away, touched that he wanted my advice on his vocation. When I did reply, I suggested that he come east for training in spiritual direction. He was ambivalent about my suggestion and wondered if the Vatican would even accept such a novel plan. It might tip the scales against his early resignation. After all, spirituality had for a long time been an interest of his. He'd read books.

"You are spiritual. But being an effective spiritual director and being spiritual are two different things. Without training you run the risk of being a guru. Have you considered enhancing your gifts?"

His face was sober as was his voice. "I'll pray about what you said. I was hoping you'd just affirm it."

Layover in Minneapolis

"A chain motel we go by will be fine. Just drop me off."

When the luggage was taken from the trunk, we both seemed sad. "Leaving Duluth, I feel like I'm leaving home." I gave him a hug of gratitude. "You made this month possible."

"Thank you for being with us, for letting me confide in you."

As soon as I'd secured a room in a motel, I collapsed on the bed. I felt touched and honored that he had confided in me. But I had little confidence that diocesan priests would spill their souls to him. What priest wants to be open and honest to someone who holds a bishop's crook? Maybe he would be an auxiliary again, but still be best friends with an ordinary? Letting go of the reins of power doesn't necessarily mean that others perceive the reins to disappear. Seekers need to feel trust and freedom with their spiritual director.

And what did he say? Reduced to the status of a lay person? Even the winners can hurt. What a maze of wonder and of dead end streets our Church provides.

Train Ride Back to Boston

"Farwell Heartland!" I whispered, as the train found enough get-up-and-go to leave the station in Minneapolis. "Is that the Mississippi?" I asked the conductor as he took my ticket.

"It sure is, ma'am. The mighty Miss."

Growing quiet within, I let the magnificent Mississippi River captivate me. Its breadth and slow-moving water silenced and calmed me. Across the river were cliffs, called bluffs out here. Around a bend, thick with greenery evocative of the South, were marshes, lilies, low-hanging trees. The rocking motion of the train brought reveries of the journey.

"I'll bring a bottle of champagne to Logan Airport, smash it against the plane, and christen your trip as a Month on Mission!" That promise and fervor from George at the beginning of my journey had transformed Pick-Up Sticks into a cross-country adventure. It seemed as if my luggage wasn't in the rack above my head; it was stored inside me, packed with all the identities I'd met this past month. It was hard to keep them all straight. A bishop could be a bishop or an archbishop or an auxiliary. There were laywomen who fasted before Communion, but nuns who didn't. Actually, some nuns only wanted to be "Sisters." Could they be women religious? Would that cover both?

There were Jesuits who could be ordained; there were laywomen with equal preparation who couldn't. The shabby southwestern Catholic family in Denver singing "Puff the Magic Dragon" and a choir of one-hundred voices in the Milwaukee basilica singing hymns in perfect harmony. Campus ministers, hospital chaplains, directors of religious education. Pastoral associates like Betty, who had to solicit food from the pantry for the poor to feed her own family. Peggy, who sings an ordination litany at a lectern from which she can never preach. *No! We're more than ecclesial identities! We are not Church 'personnel.' We are people.* And my heart, crowded with all of us, felt that luggage lodged within me. Do we feel stuck *in* the Church, or do we feel stuck *with* the Church?

In my seat I prayed. *God, replace my obsession with Church with nostalgia for the beauty I saw on my pilgrimage*: the Rockies, the Great Lakes, the Mississippi, the benches beneath trees at the retreat house in Duluth. Finally I fell asleep.

When my beloved New England came into view, I ached to be with George. In an almost empty train car, I could look through the windows on both sides at old and charming Connecticut. On my left were faded, antique brick buildings; on my right were the horizon and the blue ocean. I wanted to shout through the sound system, "I'm home! I did it! And I heard God in my heart. You took the Mayflower down the Mississippi!"

15

SYNOD ON THE LAITY

Massachusetts, Ohio, Italy, 1980s

In two tight rows we sat scrunched together in a classroom on the second floor of the Weston building. Our heads moved from left to right as though we were at a tennis game. The man speaking was explaining the box on the table to our right. I did understand his first sentence, "This is your computer." *I have two master's degrees. I should understand the next sentence and the many that are sure to follow.*

I envisioned the box growing bigger, then shrinking down to the size of a shoe box, then to a strawberry box. Then I opened the window behind the table and flung it away. I imagined the clunk as it hit the street.

Finally, he stopped speaking except to say what they all say, "Any questions?" A whole schoolroom was given over to this box and its identical twin. Along with a copy machine. We were expected to use them. *I never really figured out the rhythm method, so how am I supposed to figure out how to use this new-fangled thing?*

For the first time in a long time, I became totally sexist, only entering the room if a male professor was already there. At home George actually suggested that we buy our own computer. "You can practice here. Good Lord, you're halfway through your book and still banging on a typewriter." We bought one. I learned. And in 1986 my book, *Pilgrim in the Parish*, was published, but without a note of gratitude to the computer. I was startled when the book won an award. Maybe there was interest in the people in the pews. Letters of congratulation came, one from a colleague at the Washington Theological Union, saying he had interested a Baptist minister in reading the book!

At Weston, interest had increased in our contemplative Friday afternoons. The rector of the Jesuit community had generously offered the Jesuit facilities, on the other side of Harvard, for our quiet, sharing liturgy and potluck supper.

Eventually it grew to twenty-five people. A liturgy one Friday was celebrated by Henri Nouwen, who seemed to savor the interest in spirituality at Weston compared with Harvard, where he taught. Together, Henri and I served on the Boston Theological Institute's Spirituality Committee.

Continuing my ventures to the Midwest, I journeyed to Toledo, Ohio every few months. One time was to give a presentation on a major artist.

"How exceptional to have someone of El Greco's stature in a city the size of Toledo." That's how I began my talk when I was invited to give a presentation at the cathedral, because El Greco had lived in Toledo, Spain.

What struck me on that trip was the dearth of theologians in many dioceses in the western part of our country compared to my region with its plethora of theologians and institutions of higher learning. To counter this, a newly ordained priest and I put together an "Adopt a Theologian" program. There are eleven dioceses in the West, but there are no Catholic colleges, hence no Catholic theologians!

"Are you sure your eastern theologians want to be adopted?" a priest asked me.

"I don't know. But it would be good for them!"

Eastern Point Retreat House

One afternoon, while I was directing a retreat in Gloucester, Pamela and George surprised me. They had come to deliver a letter, which had come from Paulist Press; they wanted to publish my second book. We savored the good news in the company of Richard, an MIT student for whom I was a spiritual director, who was also making a retreat. He asked Pamela if she was familiar with Eastern Point. She replied, "Oh, no. I am not." She was fibbing. And as she had hoped, he offered to unveil its secrets.

I stayed for the next retreat, winning a suite at the end of a dorm hallway, where George could drive up from work and stay with me. Two letters came for me at the retreat house. One letter from Pamela revealing that she was occupied dating Richard each evening, and the other letter from Richard, who told me he was occupied each evening dating Pamela. The next year, in June, they were married; the priest who replaced my former boss at MIT officiated. During the same month, Pamela received her Master of Theological Studies degree from Weston and Richard received his Ph.D. from MIT. However, George suggested that he stop seeing his future mother-in-law for spiritual direction.

At Weston, in addition to moderating group gatherings and the Community Life Committee, I was engulfed in finding spiritual directors for laywomen and laymen students and arranging their get-togethers, which included the Friday afternoons of reflection; leading placement process sessions; planning eight-day retreats for students; and attending administrative meetings.

My prayer was full of gratitude for the students, especially the younger lay ones who were full of vitality and affection. It was easy to be caught up in their enthusiasm for each other and for their experience of the school.

Then two events cast dark shadows on me. The Vatican visitation was the first.

The Vatican Gathers Intelligence on Weston

Throughout the year, the Vatican was sending a delegation of American bishops to "visit" various theology schools; suspicion was rearing its ugly head, again. Teaching at the Queen of Peace Seminary had trained my senses for this type of hypocrisy. In advance of the visit, a six-page communiqué from the head of the visitation, Bishop John Marshall of Vermont, contained the bad news that "Students other than seminarians are generally not to be admitted into the academic program," which is "for the particular purpose of training candidates for the priesthood."

Twenty-five bishops were named to the visitation team. I hoped they wouldn't all show up at Weston. That the Vatican was a complicated entity was revealed in a statement about what would happen to the findings.

"Each report will be received first by the Prefect and Secretary (of the Congregation for Catholic Education). It will then be studied by the priest in charge of the English language desk. He will forward his report with his observations to the priest who oversees the Seminary department who in turn hands it on to the Secretary of the Congregation. Eventually a report is reviewed again by the Prefect and Secretary in light of accumulated observations . . . "

By then it will be the new millennium, I consoled myself. When the visitation came, I saw only the bishops and spoke a few words at a meeting with other administrators. But I worried about a lunch they gave to meet the lay students.

A gathering was held to hear the report from the visitation. Faculty met in one of the larger conference rooms. I held my breath until the bishops voiced their concerns: We were too chummy with Episcopalians, as we shared the same library and classrooms. Secondly, the Jesuits living in Cambridge houses actually did their own cooking. Chumminess with Episcopalians never happens. The cooking scandal of course could be solved by hiring, who else, a woman to cook for the men. But I wondered if these adjustments were for show and only applied to Jesuits.

Relieved but suspicious, I dreaded the second event. On January 11, 1984, a new archbishop of the Boston Archdiocese was named to replace Cardinal Medeiros, who had died. I was home when I heard that our new hierarchical figure would be Bishop Bernard Law. I cried. Dread filled my heart. George thought that was excessive, until I reminded him that Law was the bishop from the meetings in D.C. for the Bishops' Bicentennial. The meetings had been convened to receive input from priests, nuns, and lay ministers, but Law had silenced all discussions on birth control and homosexuality. *It may have been ten years ago, but I certainly haven't forgotten him.*

The unofficial response at Weston was, "Give him a chance." On the first of February I was briefly heartened by a quote from Law in *The Boston Globe*, "Women are equal to men" and "to deny that is a sin." Yet, in spite of Law's vigorous defense of equality, he insisted that only men be ordained to the priesthood.

On May 25, 1985, Law was made a cardinal. I was not surprised. On a trip to Vermont to visit my daughter, her husband, and our granddaughter, I often saw a snapping turtle that lived near their house. It came to me that it was like the Church. It moved with enormous slowness and when it opened its mouth, only snapped, "NO."

I viewed another natural experience that season, a herring run on Cape Cod. There was a pond beside an old mill and across the road was a stream that led uphill to the pond. Many small fish, never stopping or slowing down, rushed up the stream to their spawning ground. A small crowd of people gathered to watch their progress to the pond. We gazed at their determination for more than an hour.

Walking slowly back to the car, I felt a sense of healing. Being called to serve, in mission and in ministry, is like the uphill journey of the herrings, but to be loyal to the Call was to be as loyal as Jesus. It was a story I shared with our lay students in a homily.

During Lent I made my yearly journey to the Museum of Fine Arts and viewed *Christ after the Flagellation*, a late 17th century oil painting by Bartolomé Esteban Murillo. It spoke to me and moved my heart. Jesus, alone, half naked, skin broken by beatings, is crawling across a stone floor, reaching for his garment. He is made abject, stripped of humanity. I had to look away.

The National Association of Lay Ministry Coordinators

That May was the convening of the National Association of Lay Ministry Coordinators in Boston. In spite of my discomfort with its convention in Denver, I had gone to the next year's meeting in Cleveland. Where else could I belong? A fellow from Maryknoll was organizing the Boston gathering, and I was involved by locating speakers, some from Weston, and encouraging our lay students to reach out beyond Cambridge. At Emanuel College, we gathered.

I felt exhilarated even before the meeting of all in Boston, where seeds of revolution had burst with vitality two hundred years earlier. The burst of vitality at our NALMC gathering was to eliminate the C for Coordinators, and rename our church entity the National Association of Lay Ministers. It was a leap into vigorous maturity.

Coordinators, not surprisingly, disagreed vigorously. The laymen members refused to relent. But a vote was taken, and we became the National Association of Lay Ministers. Laywomen, it seemed, were caught between agreeing with the men yet realized most of the coordinators were nuns; caught between gender and Church identity.

Synod on the Laity, Toledo, Ohio

"Mom, how do you think you're going to change the Church just sitting in an office in Cambridge?" Tierney shook her head and curls tumbled on her shoulder. "You need to be talking to Rome."

I was stunned to silence by the guts, and naïveté, of my twenty-two year old kid. But, the Synod on the Laity came in 1987, two years later.

The Church was making preparations for the Synod on the Laity but requested very little input from the laypeople, despite being designated as the centerpiece. Joseph Fessio, a Jesuit priest, said that girls should not be altar servers and women should not be lectors. According to Fessio, these roles led the female to desire priesthood. In *Origins*, he was quoted as saying, "The woman is active in receiving from outside of her that which comes from the man and nourishing within her the new life . . . "

While in Toledo, I checked out their Diocesan Pastoral Council's activities. From 1971 to 1981 it had submitted fifty-nine proposals or position papers on topics as varied as youth, women, rural life, liturgy, spirituality, workshops for parish council training, and the elderly. But the diocese also connected to the larger body of the Church in the United States by issuing two position papers on current political issues. The first was in support of the Kennedy-Rodino Handgun Crime Control Act, which was eventually passed by Congress. The second was in opposition to the presence of U.S. military aid and military personnel in El Salvador.

There was none of this lay leadership in Boston under Cardinal Law.

Pilgrimage to Rome, October 1987

Two years after the name change, NALM united with PILLAR, a lay organization supported by the Pallottine religious order, to sponsor a journey to Rome for the Synod on the Laity in 1987. Two hundred and fifty signed up, including George, myself, a couple of Weston students, and some priests who wanted to support us. In Rome, at our first meeting with the Pallottine leadership, we were told we had to be patient. The Jesuits gave us a large space near their center where the ailing Fr. Pedro Arrupe, the former general lived. There, not only were we told again we had to be patient, but a correspondent from an Irish newspaper asked me if we had come to kidnap the Synod. It was such a stupid idea. I didn't ask him how we'd do it. A couple of European Catholics asked me who had given us permission to come. I replied that as far as I knew, Rome was a European city where anyone could visit.

Actually the city intrigued me far more than our conference, which I felt wouldn't make a pinprick of difference. Some of the American bishops at the Synod did come, including Peter Coughlin, from the Laity Council. He suggested we visit Curia offices to get a taste of the Vatican.

One morning several of us tramped off to the Office of Culture. We were asked by the priest in charge why we had come to this office. Three African-Americans from our group spoke of being alienated in white parishes. The Curia priest claimed that the world of culture was changing at such fantastic speed and that it was difficult for his office to keep up and devise policies.

I asked if they had considered inviting lay Catholics working in those fields to come to Rome and help them. This time he didn't tell us to be patient; he answered that it would be complicated to include the laypeople.

Later, resting out our hotel, I expressed my anger to George. "We aren't wanted! We 'complicate' the Church. So much easier for the Vatican if they rid themselves of the lay believers."

George's voice was soothing, "Just try to enjoy being here, sweetheart."

I did enjoy being on the balcony of our hotel room where we often viewed our nearby neighbors who didn't bother drawing their drapes in their apartments. We saw a mother embrace her child as she put him to bed, a couple dancing to a record on a phonograph, and fireworks that featured a lit up face of Lenin from a nearby Communist headquarters.

When we first arrived at the hotel on Via Cavour, we walked with the others across the street to St. Peter in Chains, and stood in front of Michelangelo's large statue of Moses. This seemed appropriate, Moses the Law Giver. I felt inebriated, like Jesus' disciples visiting churches at Pentecost. How does one remember all the names? Here in Rome I was stunned by how I was seized by the art: the Caravaggio in the St. Louis of the French, the grace at St. Mary Major, the charm at St. Agnes in Agony, and the warmth of heart at St. Maria in Trastevere.

At the first church belonging to the Society of Jesus, the Church of Gesù, I was moved by the *Triumph and Apotheosis of St Ignatius of Loyola,* the ceiling fresco by Fra Andrea Pozzo. Jesus is bending toward Ignatius. *Who is reaching to whom?* Moved to tears, I remembered many of the Jesuits who had befriended me.

Earlier in the week, I had decided to go into St. Peter's and just take a peek. Nobody just takes a peek in St. Peter's. You either go in or stay out. After I gazed at the *Pietà*, disappointment began. So many statues of popes. So many Bernini statues and many of abstractions: Justice, Prudence, Charity, and Truth. But toward the end of my visit, I saw the *Dove of the Holy Spirit*, Bernini's stained-glass window with long, straight brass rays emanating from the figure of a dove with its wings outstretched. There I was able to pray. Tears came. My heart felt such sorrow for the people of the Church. All the ache of years past stored in my heart came out. I did not feel anger, only sorrow. Sorrow for the people, sorrow for God, sorrow for the divisions and closed doors within our Church. The people of the Church are spiritually starved and the people of the world are materially starved.

Before we left Rome I went again to St. Peter's and prayed at the Holy Spirit window. Again I felt myself moved to tears and my heart open. This time I saw myself processing down the center aisle with priests who I'd known when Vatican II had been just turning the corner of the Church. Then George was with me, but I went on alone, a solitary figure who, I would know only later, was as a woman grappling with my "call" and "ministry."

The solitude of that journey lasted a long stretch down that endless aisle, but then I noticed others with me. Women from Weston, grassroots folks, our daughters, and other children we knew. Suddenly they dashed ahead of me to sit on the papal throne, laughing and playful. With a smile, I walked back down the aisle and left St. Peter's, knowing that God's work is accomplished by our being the women and men we are. Faithful, moving forward, not down, out of a sheer love for God.

Saturday, our last day in Rome, was a beautiful day. The sun seemed to be everywhere, like a mantle of grace. We spent hours outside, meeting for lunch with Weston students and with Scott who had planned our trip. Generosity of affection, like the sun, seemed everywhere, helped by wine and the faithfulness of the young men and women with us. Suddenly, I felt a strong desire for solitude, so George walked back to the hotel with our companions while I hotfooted it for the Church of St. Ignatius, which, of course, was closed for the siesta. I plunked myself down on a step to wait out the repose Rome offers. Before long an English-speaking pilgrim from Germany sat down beside me. In response to his questions, I sounded like it was my fifth trip to Rome. Soon we had more company on the steps until a Jesuit appeared and offered to open the doors for us. I settled down near the front, below the painting of Jesus and Ignatius. Gratitude flowed from my heart. When I closed my eyes, it seemed as if Jesus and Ignatius came down, each sitting on either side of me. My dearest of companions beside me. Contentment of heart flowed through me.

"Hurry up and pack," George barked when I returned to the hotel. "You've acted all week like you've been on retreat, and I've gone to all the Synod stuff."

"Maybe I have," I replied but didn't say I had regrets.

On the journey home I read the handout from the Vatican Office of Culture. The contents had been gathered mostly from conferences of faith, which were dominated by groups or high-ranking governmental personages. One response, from the Women's Conference of the United States read: "Are we convinced that we have something to give to the world and something to learn from it? . . . [W]e must also welcome the many faces of God that this culture reveals to us." *This is the spirit of Gaudium et Spes from Vatican II.*

As the plane descended into Boston, it struck me how different it would be to belong to a church only a few hundred years old instead of one with the warts, wounds, and wonder of two millenniums. Shortly before the Synod, the Pontifical Council for the Laity created a fifty-seven page guide for the Synod entitled *The Formation of the Laity*. A page and a half are devoted to a section entitled "The Formation of Lay Leaders Is an Ecclesial Reality and Responsibility." When the Vatican released its sixteen-page results of the Synod, two paragraphs were given to Ministries and Services: "All local churches owe a debt of gratitude to those lay faithful, men and women, who without the slightest hesitation have gone forth through the centuries, even to martyrdom, together with clergy and religious, to build the Church to the ends of the earth."

Cambridge

The day George and I returned from Rome, my sister-in-law Louise called to tell me that my mother was in the hospital.

"She's had hip surgery. When the ambulance brought her there, she told them not to bother you."

"Louise, why would my mother say that?"

"She said you were in Rome visiting the Pope."

"Oh, I can't believe her. Thank you so much. I'll pack my bags and leave for the hospital now."

As soon as I walked into the hospital room, my mother beamed.

"Did you tell the Pope to pray for me? Because my operation went fine! I asked the doctor if he wanted me to sing while he worked on my hip. He said that would be lovely. So I sang during my surgery."

"What did you sing?"

" I Love You Truly."

Having attended the Synod, I was invited to give several talks about it. I emphasized the realization of being part of a world Church. As word went around that nothing had really happened in Rome, I grew agitated because a great deal was happening in Rome. *Not all of it good and everyone should be on alert.*

It was good being back with the lay students, whose mood veered from high to low. The latter was especially pronounced the Monday after the Jesuit diaconate ordination when six students lined up at my door. Seeing them one by one, I heard the same message: Without being ordained, I'll be a nobody in the church. I listened. *This is not the time to ask if they felt that God was calling them to mission through ministry.*

With women students I journeyed to the Dominican retreat center in Glastonbury, not far from the ocean, for a weekend. Though it was chilly, we gathered outside to let balloons, on which we had fastened notes listing our hopes to endure, fly to heaven. Photos were taken, one that would turn into my Christmas card to send to friends and faculty.

The first evening one laywoman asked me a question that was hard to answer, "How do you know that the Holy Spirit calls you to ministry? How do you know?" *There is no simple answer.*

"If you hear or sense the same nudge again and again, and you bring it to prayer, but get no direct response, continue listening to it and stay with it, for a clearer discernment."

In one of my own prayers, I reflected on Rome and an image came to me. *Jesus is standing beside me, seeming in no hurry to do anything. We are in St. Peter's, both of us gazing up at the Holy Spirit window. Suddenly, Jesus reaches up and pushes the window open. "No!" I shout, appalled.*

"But see, I've improved it. Now we can see the heavens." He gently takes my arm, leads me to the altar, placing me behind it. Some of the women students are standing beside me. "See," he says "symbols of the Holy Spirit."

16

PAPERS AND PAMPHLETS

Cambridge, Massachusetts, 1980s

Papers and pamphlets were scattered over the Duncan Phyfe table my mother lent us when we moved to Boston. "Mom, what on earth are you doing?"

"While you were at work, I thought I'd investigate the case under your typewriter table." Her thin hand shook.

"It's a computer. Please don't touch it."

"If I could type, I might be tempted." She winked.

Mom's orthopedic surgeon had forbidden her from going back to her duplex. She was forced, against her will, to move to Belmont and into our rented apartment. George and I informed her landlady and packed up her clothes and sentimental things, but we also had to spend time at her bank; We had discovered that her savings bank book, which she kept in the butter drawer of the refrigerator, showed a large withdrawal on the date of her surgery. The bank manager sat us down to review tapes of customers at the drive-up window.

"There she is!" I shouted when I saw the face of my mother's aide, who was then contacted, arrested, and forced to give back the sum to Mom, who had never even known of the theft.

Yet Mom sulked in her room at our place. "When are my other children going to come and get me?" she asked after a few days, as she hobbled with her cane.

"You only had me, Mom. No other kids."

"How could I have been so stupid?"

Now, in our dining room she rummaged through my collection of pamphlets and newsletters. "Here's a lovely one. All the speakers are cardinals or bishops and even the pope." She handed me *The Apostolate for Family Consecration*. It advertised a set of tapes, not one by a married person.

"This one puzzles me—The Association for the Rights of Catholics. As Americans, we have rights but not as Catholics." She handed me a copy of its publication, *Light*, with its lead article, "A Plan to Promote Democracy in Germany." *Could there be a wider gap than these two groups?*

When George came in she told him, "I was invited to join one of these clubs," sweeping her hand over the table.

"Mom, they aren't clubs, they're organizations," I said.

George asked, "Did you join any clubs, Blanch?"

"No, I didn't need the Daughters of Isabella club. The parish was enough for me. I didn't want that nonsense."

"I'm going to start dinner." I rushed to the kitchen.

She wouldn't let it go. Scooping up corn with a spoon, "George," she asked, "did you belong to the Knights of Columbus club?"

"No, in Northampton I belonged to the Holy Name club." Under the table, his foot nudged mine.

While they spent that evening in the living room watching television, I tried to make sense of what my mother's hand had scattered on the table. "The Cursillo," I murmured. "Imagine calling that a club!" When George made his in New Hampshire Cursillo weekend it had more impact than his years in Holy Name.

Other organizations and networks had an emphasis on spirituality: the Charismatics; Contemplative Outreach, which reported that Fr. Thomas Keating's system of Centering Prayer had attracted 10,000 Catholics; and Friends of Silence.

Some of what I'd collected was more practical. Like Marriage Encounter and Teams of Our Lady, which in its pamphlet recounted its origin in France in 1947 to bring couples together, because alone they "are weak, unprepared, and beset by the strife of daily life." George and I could profit from this "club."

The Beginning Experience, in another pamphlet, said it was for "widowed, separated, and divorced persons making a new beginning" with chapters in seven countries, including the United States with many groups in thirty-two states.

As my mother hobbled past me on her way to bed, she said to the air, "My daughter's getting too big for her britches."

Spurred by her remark, I lined the bottom of the case under my desk with catalogs from a couple of Catholic colleges and some magazines that seldom featured any news about all these associations. On top of these I put *The Catholic Worker* with an article by laywoman Dorothy Day, "The Faces of Poverty." Before putting away papers from the St. Joan's International Alliance, I glanced through them and found that as early as 1961, it had urged through a resolution for a diaconate as an independent ministry open to women as well as men. The following year, the French organization met in Orleans and urged more lay advisers to the Synod.

"Almost finished?" George asked as he passed me on his way to bed. "From the looks of the number of clubs you have, is there any need for parishes?"

"Quite a mix. I'll be in soon."

But before I gave up, I found and almost fondled material from the National Pastoral Musicians Conference where I had given the keynote address two years earlier. In memory I gazed again at the sea of faces and remembered what I'd said about the film *Amadeus*. The onset of Vatican II, I had said, evoked dialogue, collegiality, and collaboration. The creativity and originality of Mozart was symbolized in our time by the emergence of a kind of folk music that enabled the whole congregation to sing and, by participation, to sense at hand God's immanence. On the other hand, Salieri's faithfulness to tradition had not been abandoned as the formality of other musical liturgical offerings enable a sense of God's transcendence by more classical forms of church music.

As I set aside this set of remembrances to show my mother, I spotted a flyer from the Office of Worship for the Archdiocese of St. Louis, where I was once invited to give a presentation for its once-every-four-years profile of a praying church. George had told me not to get any funny ideas, as the conference was to be held at a hotel called Henry VIII. Spirituality was addressed by others; my topic was "People in the Pews: Hopes and Hungers." An added treat was a special interest session in which I showed slides of the Vineyard's inclusion of community-made creative arts in the liturgy.

Over the course of the year, we muddled over what to do with all my mother's furniture from her house, as we had no room in our apartment. We began looking for alternatives. Our dearest friends, Don and Barbara, urged us to consider retiring to the Berkshires. One evening Don called, "I found a place for you. It's a two-family house in South Lee."

George and I drove west that Saturday, and in spite of pouring rain, Don met us in the backyard. We were surrounded by a dozen tall trees near a river.

"Let's buy it," I said.

"We haven't seen the inside," George remarked.

"I don't care . . . I'm sick of penny-sized lawns in Boston."

When Mom came to see it, she found it boring. "There's nothing but trees to look at. I like our place in Boston better."

One afternoon, when I came home from Weston, she said, "I don't know what you do at work all day."

"People talk with me about God."

"Why talk about God when you can talk to God."

I decided to show her my photo album with pictures of the students. She'd point to one woman then another. "Is she a nun?" I'd affirm it and she'd find another. "A nun?"

Finally she said, "I wish I had been a nun."

Two days later, George came home from work and told me he was arranging interviews for us to facilitate my mother's entrance into an adult day-care program. At first she complained that the others there were too old, but after two weeks, she loved it.

One afternoon, she came home and said, "There were Negro people there today because their place is being fixed. In all my eighty-seven years I've never been in a room with Negroes. Don't know how I feel about it."

Eighty-seven years in New England, sounds more like Nebraska. "Mom, now we say black, not Negro."

"How cruel! Reminding them of their skin color."

A week later, Mom claimed she hoped they stayed where she was. "They like what I like, singing and religion!"

Participating with the other seniors sweetened her mood, especially one day when she claimed to have danced with President Kennedy. "Mom, because of your hip you can't dance," I reminded her.

"Well, I did! You think I dream up my adventures."

It was no dream. A few days later George brought home a news-paper clipping with a large picture of my mother and Joe Kennedy, the president's nephew who was running for Congress, dancing a jig. "She's only been here a year and she's better known in the area than you are," George teased.

In spite of dancing the jig and claiming credit for Joe Kennedy's congressional win, my mother continued to slow down until the di-rector of her day care center said she wanted to put her on a list for a nursing home in Cambridge, as her mobility and incontinence were worsening. Others were ahead of her on the list, but Blanche was so sociable that they accelerated her entrance. She was as mad about moving into the nursing home as she had been about moving to Belmont.

After two days in the home, Mom had a mouthful of praise. "See these sheets—look at how white they are. The ones you put on my bed always looked worn out. See these bars on my bed—at your place in that skimpy twin bed I was always afraid I'd fall on the floor. And I have my own TV."

I left the nursing home with a big grin pasted on my face.

On one visit, Mom was watching *The Oprah Winfrey Show*, which featured a segment on alcoholism. I said, "We know what that is."

"What on earth are you talking about?"

"Your husband, Tommy. My father."

"Oh, the less said about him the better."

We had not talked about my father in years. One night I stopped in rather late to visit Mom. I came by her bed at the end of the room near the windows, then stopped. She was praying, "Dear God, thank you for the beautiful day. The trees are pretty and the pond is peaceful like I feel. Thank you, Lord."

I turned around and walked down the corridor. Although my posture was normal, I felt totally bent over. In the car, I put my arms on the steering wheel, then my head on top of them. *If I were bedridden for almost a year as she has been since she broke her other hip, there is no way I could offer such gratitude to God.*

Mom's prayer of gratitude lingered with me during the following days. I remembered the time I walked from my room as a child toward her and Daddy's room. She was on her knees by the bed clutching her novena booklets, with tears streaming down her face, begging God to stop my father's drinking. I stepped back to my room but never forgot her intensity. She had a relationship with God that was primary. Besides novenas, my mother cherished the rosary, visits to the French church on her way back from the mill, and the Stations of the Cross on Fridays. But she also cherished the Forty Hours Devotion, Vespers, and Benediction of the Blessed Sacrament.

Adoration is what these provided. Has that been lost in the Vatican II Church? Along with a sense of the Trinity? It dawned on me that the French church around the corner was where I made a visit after school, lit a candle at the Mary altar, and said the stations as well as prayed to God in a personal way. My spiritual identity was formed there. The insight surprised me.

The Irish church, over a mile away, where we "belonged" because my father was Irish, was where I was baptized and made my First Communion, and where I went each Saturday morning for catechism. I remember learning the catechism and being punched in the back by a nun at Mass to kneel up straight. I was so famished from fasting I thought I'd faint every Sunday. Now I saw that the Irish church gave me my ecclesial identity. It taught me what it meant to be a Catholic believer among other believers, but the French church gave me my personal affection for God.

The last time I saw my mother, it was near Easter. I was on my way to Eastern Point to direct a retreat. I stopped to visit with her in the nursing home. She was holding a small wooden cross and we talked about Jesus. "Jesus," she said, "He means so much to me." She began singing, "I Have Decided to Follow Jesus." *Mom, Jesus loves you more than you know.*

While I was on the retreat, the nursing home called. My mother had passed away, during her afternoon nap. Although I was sad, I felt thankful that she had gone peacefully.

Her funeral in Easthampton was beautifully celebrated by Tom Kane, a Paulist priest who taught at Weston. There were very few guests at her funeral; most of her friends, siblings, and cousins had already passed on. *That can happen if you live to be ninety-one.*

17

PREACHING TO PEOPLE, PRIESTS, AND BISHOPS

Virginia, New York, Massachusetts, Ohio, 1988

Hampton Roads, Virginia

The Peace Event of 1988 was a series of gatherings structured to promote peace throughout the world. Initiated by Bishop Walter Sullivan of the Richmond, Virginia diocese, the meetings were held in Hampton Roads, home of the world's largest naval base and 15 percent of the nation's military personnel.

The final day was an Advent event reflecting on "The Challenge of Peace." At this crowded meeting, I gave a presentation on "Voices of the Parish." For the first, and last, time I spoke about how patriotism had affected my father. I explained that after the invasion of Normandy, he attempted suicide. He came home from the hospital at Fort Devens, and kept mumbling over and over, "They did D-Day without me." My dad had received a dishonorable discharge because he was an alcoholic, which was kept secret from friends and neighbors, and it was the most agonizing time in my life as a child. As I gave my talk, I was stunned by the eyes of the adolescent boys glued on me as I told my tale of patriotism.

Brooklyn, New York

After my second book, *Pilgrims in This World*, was published, my career giving talks and workshops expanded. I was invited to speak at the Diocesan Pastoral Congress for Brooklyn. There were forty-two presentations, which centered on liturgy and religious education; mine was the only workshop about mission.

Gloucester, Massachusetts

George and I gave a weekend retreat at the Eastern Point on how laypeople incorporate their mission through their work. Many participants surprised us by traveling far to attend. Having grown up in an elite college town, George spoke about his first job after college at a meat packing plant, where he met black and Hispanic men for the first time in his life. On the retreat participants could sign up to meet individually, with George or me. George looked at the sign-up sheet in confusion, "More people have signed up to meet me than you?"

"What a treat," I said.

"But what do I say to them?"

"Nothing. You listen to them. Probably none of the clergy in their parish have ever asked them to speak about their work, but work is one place where mission can take place."

Toledo, Ohio

During a visit with my friend, Bishop Jim in Toledo, I had discovered his creative approach to parishes in his diocese. Each parish had lay ministers who served as director of religious education, youth ministers, business manager, director of music, and director of liturgy. A priest, referred to as chaplain, would oversee two or three parishes. Jim hired local lay ministers, not theological school graduates.

When I expressed my disappointment and shock that he had not sought out these students, he countered my objection by saying it wasn't realistic.

"The last thing you grads want is to live in the boondocks of Ohio."

Was Jim right? One area where I knew he was wrong was the general lack of focus on spirituality within the parishes.

I referred to the *Baltimore Catechism* from 1901.

"In 1901 it says—"

"1901—start of the twentieth century? We're almost ready for the twenty-first century."

"Now listen to Question 1098."

Jim rolled his eyes.

"Q. 1098. Is there any other means of obtaining God's grace than the sacraments? A. There is another means of obtaining God's grace, and it is prayer.

"Q. 1104. Is prayer necessary to salvation? A. Prayer is necessary to salvation, and without it no one having the use of reason can be saved."

His hand was over his mouth, hiding a smile. "There are twenty-six answers on prayer," I bragged. "Lately, on many of the retreats I have directed, so many people come too intent on exploring the latest fad of personality tests—Enneagram numbers, Myers-Briggs scores, color wheels, dream analysis. To them, God is second fiddle!"

We both laughed. We each knew how much mission as well as ministry meant to each of us. *Twenty-five years after Vatican II, the Church still hasn't figured out how the post-conciliar Church could work, but differences are cropping up everywhere. From an institution's point of view, that indicates chaos and confusion, but for Americans, evolution is a healthy thing.*

18

COUNTING THE PEOPLE IN

Massachusetts and Connecticut, Early 1990s

According to an article in the *National Catholic Reporter*, the Weston's placement program was the only program devoted to preparing lay students for careers in the ministerial profession. I had put my heart and soul into creating this placement process. I did this mostly because I was frightened that after they had spent so much time, money, and spiritual engagement, our lay students would face a void of working opportunities.

Resume preparation was, of course, part of the process in addition to volunteer experience and spiritual growth activities. Each year, we sent a packet of student resumes to the diocesan offices. We also did mock interviews and alumni returned to share their work experiences.

Eastern Point Retreat House

Students of Weston made a retreat together at Eastern Point, which had a beautiful setting on the ocean. Brian McDermott, S.J., a fellow professor at Weston and I were spiritual directors for the eight-day retreat.

The students tolerated the silence observed on the retreats well. However, when it was time to plan the liturgy, a few students extended their sessions, savoring the chance to chat. It was clear that they had a deep desire to do what they were often denied the opportunity; design the service, which connects God to her people.

There were a few lay students who questioned their call to ministry. I gave them scripture readings in which disciples were sent to minister. At the end of the week, a layman came to me with wonder on his face.

"At last year's retreat, all I did was pray for what I wanted God to do for me. This year it was searching for what I could do with God."

Retreat directors were blessed with phones in our rooms and one afternoon mine rang. It was a fellow asking if I might be interested in accepting a grant from a foundation. He was approaching me because the director of the National Association of Lay Ministers had turned it down. As a leader of the Spiritual Committee for the NALM, I was next in line! *Perfect timing! Summer is almost within reach. School will soon be closed and I'll have time to design a project!*

Conducting a Study of God's People: Laypeople and Lay Ministers

While leading a ministerial workshop in a Connecticut parish with another woman, I conceived of a project that could be funded by the grant. At the conclusion of the workshop, we were reading over the participants' response forms. One was from a layman in his sixties, who had volunteered in the church all of his adult life. He commented that our workshop was the first time that anyone had asked him about his relationship with God. He would be going home and reflecting on that inclusion. It was crystal clear: The NALM venture would explore the spirituality of laypeople.

There were two components:

- Conduct in-depth conversations with parishioners at a local church.
- Distribute queries to NALM members regarding their spiritual supports.

We would have the responses analyzed by a professor of sociology and by three professional lay ministers.

The final element of the project would be a compilation of the results into a report, delivered to the members of the NALM. These could be used as a reference for its future endeavors. Also, a book on the interviews with parishioners would be published.

The Spiritual State of Laypeople: A Connecticut Parish

Our interviews revealed a lot about the spiritual life and connection that parishioners felt to their local church.

Many mature parishioners described their difficulty in adjusting to the changes at church prompted by Vatican II. For some, it took a few years. As one woman said, "Letting go of eating fish on Friday was tough. Jesus died on Good Friday." For another the Mass was too busy now, leaving no time for private prayer: "You're thinking all the time."

In contrast, a few of the participants who were born post Vatican II, described their spiritual experiences. One woman sensed God when she was engaged in liturgical dance. A young man attending a Catholic college felt God's presence during sharing time in a small Bible group attended by others his age.

The lay respondents had a wide range of striking descriptions of their religious experiences. One man revealed his feeling of God's presence when his family came close together during the wake and funeral of their father. Another lay minister described savoring peace and quiet while visiting a tree farm.

Some respondents shared events that were life changing. One man experienced firsthand the courage and faith that is takes to live a life following God's desires and valuing morals. After he revealed a theft by an employee at his job, he was demoted and shunned.

A woman who had given birth to six children in ten years had to have a hysterectomy. Afterward, she felt a great burden and fear lifted from her heart and saw the necessary surgery as a blessing in disguise.

Direct engagement with Jesus characterized some of the lay experiences. One woman wrote the following for her response:

"I have been belaboring my efforts to overcome faults, mine and others, to establish a holy and just society, to push and push for balance and peace . . . Finally I gave up. I just said, 'Oh Lord, I give up. I just want to be ordinary.' Then I experienced Jesus laughing and saying, 'At last.' I felt a great burden lifted."

Another woman was praying in her bedroom one afternoon and reflecting on the crucifix. She was challenged with a new baby, the hospitalization of her husband, moving her elderly parents to a new home, and then came the last straw, her refrigerator broke. "I shouted at Jesus on the crucifix, 'Enough is enough. I can't take any more of this!' Suddenly I felt peace for the first time in months. 'Thanks!' I shouted to Jesus."

Members of the NALM

The second portion of the NALM study observed any spiritual supports available to lay ministers. The responses from the lay ministers revealed what I had anticipated; lay ministers had a thirst for spiritual direction and to attend retreats, but they had little time and energy for either. Due to the shortage of priests, lay ministers were doing a lot of the ministry that priests used to do. *There are many, many workaholics in the field of lay ministry.*

In reviewing the completed surveys, I observed that many of the responses were reminiscent of the values commonly referred to as "the web of life," in which God's people are pilgrims who live fully in the world. This term referred to the Church and God's people as intimately related to the world. Vatican II explored this theology in its *Pastoral Constitution on the Church in the Modern World.* The Church is "a community composed of people united in Christ who are directed by the Holy Spirit . . . " Through our existence we share "joys and hopes and the sorrows and anxieties of people today."

After compiling the findings, we distributed them through the Secretariat for the Laity and Family Life to the National Conference of Catholic Bishops in Washington, D.C.

The Media of the Institutionalized Church

The editor of my previous books, which had been published by a Catholic publishing company, had seen a copy of the report and was very interested in a book based on the study. However, when I submitted my proposal, the publishing company turned it down. I was shocked. The publishers told me, "These laypeople aren't prophetic. They're just run of the mill." *These people are the bedrock of our church. Stop ignoring them!*

The Vatican Does Reconnaissance on the Laypeople

When I returned to Weston, a new and exciting semester was beginning. A teaching position had opened up when David Flaming, S.J., who taught a practicum in spiritual direction had left. I wondered who would replace him. "Why not you?" asked Dean Smith. (We had worked together when I helped him set up the administrative part of the course.)

Next, I received a letter from the Vatican. Msgr. Peter Coughlin, Tierney's friend and a member of the Pontifical Council for the Laity in Rome, wanted to come visit me. After George and I met the Monsignor's plane, we took him to a seafood restaurant in Boston where cherrystones and oysters on ice were waiting. By the end of a wonderful dinner, we were all on a first name basis and having a great time. After we dropped Peter at one of the lovely Weston College residency buildings in Cambridge, George asked me, "Why is such a personable and engaging priest like Peter letting himself be locked up in the Vatican?" I didn't know and Peter never said, but he eventually told me that the days of harmony were coming to an end in the curial offices.

Peter was very interested to hear about my experiences and opinions of Cardinal Law, but as a lowly lay minister, I refrained from answering some of his inquiries. However, I did give him a picture of Law from the cover of the archdiocesan newspaper; the cardinal was posing as Christ carrying a lamb on his shoulders. Peter made a Cheshire cat smile. It appeared he knew what the rest of us did not yet put together.

Cardinal Law had managed to get his own bishops from Boston promoted to head other Catholic dioceses, including Palm Beach, Green Bay, New Orleans, South Bend, and Brooklyn. *As a general rule, the appointment of bishops is done by a council in the Vatican.*

19

LEADING LAYPEOPLE TO THE FRONT

Boston and Washington, D.C., 1990s

In 1990, *The Atlantic* magazine published a twenty-eight-page article, "The Hand That Would Shape Our Souls," by layman Paul Wilkes. Wilkes wrote of the effort by the Catholic operation to develop the spiritual formation of lay ministers and priests who serve the church, which was in contrast to other denominations.

At the same time, I was invited by WGBH, Boston's PBS affiliate, to be its spiritual specialist for *The Group*, a weekly discussion program. My presence was sporadic, as the program didn't always focus on religion, but it was stimulating to "share the stage" with Harvey Cox, professor at Harvard Divinity School, and other religious leaders.

Teaching the Practicum in Spirituality

At Weston, Dean Smith asked me to teach the Practicum in Spiritual Direction, which also included students from the Boston Theological Institute. Many students were also curious about my process.

In class, I asked "If you are in Boston and the person you're directing lives in Worcester, what do you do?"

One young priest quickly responded with his own question. "You're using geography as a metaphor, right?"

"That's right." I replied with a smile.

"Then you go to Worcester!" he answered with pride and enthusiasm.

The other students nodded as they also realized a crucial part of spiritual direction.

You have to discover where your client is with God, and not teach your client where God is.

When I assigned a book by Pierre Wolff, a former Catholic priest who was now an Episcopalian, I asked the class what they thought of the title, *May I Hate God?*

Two priests from different religious orders immediately pointed out that it was always sinful to hate God. In the back of the room, a middle-aged Protestant minister stood up. "When I learned that my son was killed in a car accident, I went out in the backyard to the rubbish bins, shook my fist up to God and shouted, 'I hate you!'" That quieted everybody. *Now they see how wonderfully diverse believers are.*

In my class, Fr. Timothy, an Irish Jesuit, helped me plan a weekly Lenten program on Wednesday afternoons. Timothy suggested we ask faculty members to share their spiritual lives. *That's bold. But ask away.*

We asked and only two accepted, but on the first afternoon many came, actually filling the conference room. Lay students, women religious, and Jesuit students attended. Occasionally, faculty members came and shared their own spiritual life, which had rarely been done previously. I began to invite lay alumni to return and share their experiences of working as campus ministers, hospital chaplains, and parish leaders.

The National Association of Lay Ministers

At the spacious John B. Hynes Veterans Memorial Convention Center in Boston, I attended the consecration of Rev. Barbara Harris to be the first woman bishop in the Episcopal Diocese of Massachusetts. For me the experience was poignant but also prudent; somewhere along the way, I had lost my desire for ordination. And soon after, I was asked and accepted the position as executive director of the National Association of Lay Ministers. I felt a validation that I was on a path with God to expand lay ministry.

Attending the National Catholic Conference of Bishops

As the head of a Catholic organization, I was able to get a precious pass to the November meeting of the National Catholic Conference of Bishops in Washington, D.C. The pressroom full of journalists reporting on our stories was stimulating, but not as much as the bishops' discussion of whether or not to allow women to preach. *You're a little late. I've delivered more than seventy-five sermons—at MIT, Weston, and retreat houses.*

Some of the bishops' remarks were practical: "Are you saying that if Mother Theresa came to visit the U.S., we would forbid her from giving a homily at mass?" "Don't you want Dolores Leckey, whom you entrust with our Laity and Marriage Office, to preach?"

The vote on allowing women to preach stunned me. The margin, while not narrow, was within shouting distance of a win. Women would not be able to preach.

At the conference I visited with my old friends from Ohio, Bishop Jim and Bishop Albert. Albert was excited about an Advent project that he had mandated to bring people together across parish lines.

One parish would connect with two other parishes for Advent services, taking turns weekly. "The pastors who like their own turf aren't thrilled, so I've hired women religious to moderate their planning meetings." I cheered him on and told him the idea was "beautifully collaborative." *He's breaking the isolation and ownership of individualist parishes and creating community!*

Defying the Bishops and Preaching During Holy Week

Two months later, I received a letter from a prelate who obviously hadn't heard of the bishops' rejection of women preaching. Fr. John, a priest in a suburb of Worcester, asked me to give a homily at every Holy Week service. Because the parish was a forty-five-minute drive from Belmont, he suggested that I stay in the rectory. The former was a blessing; the latter was a challenge.

After each service we went directly to our separate bedrooms for the evening. *I miss George, but at least I get to talk with him at the end of each day, and hear about his stories from his job. But how on earth do diocesan priests stand living in an empty rectory?*

I was warned that the attendance at the Holy Week services would drop off after Palm Sunday. Instead it increased, delighting the pastor and me. The successful and fulfilling week culminated in a wonderful Easter Mass, back in Belmont with George.

20

A JOURNEY THROUGH EUROPE

Northern Europe, 1991

Learning the history of the courageous
Protestants and Catholics
of Post-War Germany.

Itinerary gripped in one hand, boarding pass in the other, I boarded my flight to Germany from Logan Airport. Even before finding my seat on the plane, I bent my head and took a few deep breaths to shift my thoughts from teaching and tending to the lay students, to my pilgrimage. I closed my eyes and forced myself to admit that I was on my way to a country I'd never seen. A country my father had fought against, in the two World Wars. As the mighty transport lifted itself and all of us on board into the sky, I gripped the arms of my seat. *Would the wars that Germany had started evoke resentments?*

When the flight attendants finally offered drinks, I sighed and told myself there was nothing to do but let the journey pull me ahead. I was looking forward to seeing Max Schmidt again. He was a German Jesuit, one of the few international Catholics who attended the National Association of Lay Ministers' annual conference, and he had invited me to witness the ministry in his native Germany.

Munich

As I disembarked in Munich, I spied Max, looking eager for our joint venture to begin. Smiling, with blond hair and a beard well groomed, he seemed to give away tension only in his eyes, which were on each side of a deep crease. Celibate life made his age uncertain, as is often the case.

Max was thrilled that I had arrived in time for Corpus Christi, a three-day holiday! The Munich parade, as I called it, was astounding. Bishops in full regalia, nuns in Vatican I habits, altar boys in scarlet surplices, and choirs dressed in various outfits. The procession advertising Bavaria as Catholic went on and on. I whispered to Max, "What do Jews think of all this?"

"There aren't many Jews in Munich," he replied.

Hmm. That's a rather strange wording of it.

Max seemed to read my thoughts. "You Americans make too much of the camps."

As we mingled with people in the crowd, a married deacon told me that the younger women in the community argued all the time with the older women. They were loyal to Vatican II and deplored the outdated devotional practices that the older women tried to force upon everyone.

Freiburg

From Munich, Max drove to Freiburg, an old town with many churches and a cathedral, near the Alsace wine region. I stayed with Dr. Gottlieb Brunner, the head of the diocesan office of theology, and his American wife. I visited a parish church nearby, which had a spacious communal garden and a wall decorated with beautiful paintings made by children from the community. When I raved about it, Dr. Gottlieb's wife explained that they were losing their full-time priest. "But it is no problem. We have over twenty small groups. We'll manage with a sub."

As we traveled in the opposite direction to Leipzig, Max tutored me in some of the realities of the former and newly freed East Germany. "We used to call it the GDR and we remember the uprisings as the *Wende*." We flew through what had once been the headquarters for border permission. Later I sighted many cows in a meadow.

"Look how pleasant that meadow is, Max."

"It's a collective farm. Better not praise it."

Leipzig

As we entered Leipzig, I frowned. Black smoke from coal had drifted out and concealed the city's buildings no matter how tall they were. When we reached the apartment building where my hosts lived, they were waiting outside: Anna, with rosy cheeks and flyaway blonde hair, and Karl, tall and strong muscled. Max and I followed them up the seven flights of stairs to their apartment with a long hall and closed doors on each side.

We ate on the coffee table in the living room, as there was no room for a table in the kitchen. There was no sink in the bathroom and no telephone in the whole building, not even a pay phone. For ten years Anna and Karl had been on a list for a phone. Karl, though trained as a teacher, was forced to take a factory job, one that enabled them to have a tape recorder, a television, and an electric mixer.

"Since the *Wende* we've been able to buy kiwi fruit!" Karl shouted.

After lunch Max left and we took a drive around the city in their Renault. Passing one tall building, Anna pointed to it. "Twenty-five stories where people live. They have an elevator. But it's broken." She laughed. "So, seven floors is nothing."

That night I met joyful Catholic college students who still had a hard time believing that after they graduated they could travel anywhere. After two hours of the students sharing their stories, there was one young man who had not spoken at all. His eyes constantly averted mine. I put down my pen and closed my notebook.

"Can you tell me your story? I asked.

"The *Wende*." Bitterness clung to his words. "Before the *Wende* there were always people to tell you what to do. Now I wake up in the morning and I'm confused. Should I do this? Should I do that? Nobody will tell me what to do." His voice was vibrating. "What you Americans treasure— freedom—is only agony for me."

Back in Anna and Karl's apartment, with their three children off to sleep, I opened the sofa bed and climbed in with the words of the college student an echo within me. *The* Wende . . . *Vatican II . . . Some folks want to be told what to do, but others want to have a say.*

The next morning Karl and Anna took me to see what had been the Soviet headquarters for spying on the citizens of Leipzig in the GDR. I found myself standing next to a mannequin in an ill-fitting Stasi uniform. Lists on white paper lay on surveillance equipment that secret agents had used to stalk neighbors, friends, and even family for the Ministry for State Security—the Stasi.

A moment later we walked toward the foyer with its heightened, domed ceiling where we met Gisela, a stocky woman with a plain face.

"I am a nurse, the mother of two sons and, with my husband, I serve on the parish council." She sat on the stone bench close to me and went on. "My sons were called up for GDR military service, but they requested non-combatant service. Accused of being pacifists instead of patriots for the Soviets, they were beaten and thrown into prison. After two years they were sent back home, too broken for work."

Instead of fear restraining Gisela and her husband, the torment of their sons pushed them into risks by joining an ecumenical group involved in the *Wende*. They had gone to a church, which was surrounded by soldiers and blood hungry dogs.

Describing the *Wende*, color came into her cheeks. She smiled. "A few days after the *Wende* took hold, a small group of us marched down here and stormed the Stasi headquarters and demanded the surrender of the Secret Police. And it worked! So here we are."

A heartfelt gratitude grabbed me and I hugged her.

"You'd do the same. It's our mission as Catholics," she said.

The next day as I left Karl and Anna for a train to Munich, Karl asked about the places I would visit in the former West Germany. I listed them and asked, "Have you been to Nuremberg and Munich?"

"No. We crossed the border once to go where my father is buried."

"And once to Regensburg!" Anna added.

"How can that be?" Confusion addled my thoughts. "Do you mean that I visited more places in one month than you've seen in your *life?* In your *own* country? "

"You've known freedom, Virginia. First hand."

Salzburg

A helpful porter found an empty compartment for my jaunt to Salzburg. As the train slipped out of the station, I loosened my shoes, fell back on the upholstered seat, and felt relief on leaving the former GDR. I stretched out and closed my eyes. Took deep breaths. I knew then how much I needed the reprieve I hoped Salzburg intended to provide.

When the Alps finally loomed on the horizon with a proximity that called for tidying myself and my belongings, I gave what the sight of them demanded—wondrous reverence. The Berkshires, my beloved mountains, were round-shouldered hills compared to the proud peaks of the Alpine vista before me. To give it deserved respect, I hurried to the dining car. Such beauty merited a feast.

Twilight had deepened on our arrival at the Salzburg *Hauptbahnhof.* I rushed to the general delivery window and picked up an envelope with the key to the flat I was borrowing. The apartment was cozy, but my appreciation turned to awe. From the picture window an Alpine peak, shaded purple in the twilight, reigned over all.

What I wanted the days in Salzburg to be were a furlough from the front lines of battle and sorrow. It was such a relief to be away from Germany.

In the morning I walked to the cathedral, passing clean bright buildings with stores and concert halls. *Stunning. Beautiful after the mourning appearance of East Germany. No wonder the powers in charge refused to let the Leipzig citizens visit.*

The cathedral was not overdone and seemed to embody it's most famous citizen, Mozart. The pastor who celebrated mass was unassuming and soft-spoken while the choir and the instruments lifted us into prayer. For the first time in days, my heart hummed with peace.

Wurstberg

The quiet time in Austria hardly prepared me for the whirlwind Max had arranged for our days back in Germany. Sometimes I didn't even know where we were, but I was learning. In the Wurstberg Diocese, due to the shortage of priests, some empty rectories became homes for lay pastoral assistants or pastoral associates. There was some complaining, though, because men were favored and parishioners considered the lay leaders as priests. *Live in the rectories! The American Church is behind the times.*

In Wurstberg I met a woman named Heidi, who struck me as having the disposition of an early feminist back home. She had leadership qualities by nature and encouraged spiritual formation for all lay ministers. Tall and attractive, and married with children, she took us on a tour of the chancery and a Catholic senior residence that to me resembled the Ritz-Carlton. Everyone greeted others with "God is good."

Nuremberg

Then Max and I were off to the old town section of Nuremberg. I learned that fourteen independent groups had laypersons working full-time in the chancery office for the diocese. Max explained this. "A parish is not the priest. A parish is the people."

Bonn

The next morning Max took me to Bonn, where I met with a woman who headed the National Pastoral Council.

"In America, your peace pastoral should never have been launched by bishops."

"But we don't even have a National Pastoral Council."

"I know. But how can your laypeople exercise leadership? All those independent national groups you Americans have. Where is their impact? How can they be sustained?"

Munich

The next day we returned to Munich, after crisscrossing all of Germany. My last meeting would be to offices on a crowded central street. Max introduced me to Stefan Weber, an administrator who worked with several German parish councils. His comments regarding the influence of Vatican II in Germany lifted my respect for German Catholics even higher than it already was.

"For Vatican II, we introduced the idea of establishing both national and diocesan pastoral councils. From what I hear in your country, you have many parish councils. Here we did them under the assistance and oversight of the diocesan pastoral councils, which were already well established."

"In the United States, many of our parish councils flounder. They don't get help from anywhere. In New England there is little diocesan help,"

"But as *Germans*, we had to instill democracy. You were the war victors and didn't have that burden. Though John Courtney Murray was a great exception for ecumenism."

Stefan knows his theologians!

The next morning, it was off to the train station. I thanked Max profusely for being my shepherd on my pilgrimage.

Brussels

In a dining room in a Brussels hotel I looked up and there he was. Our rendezvous had been planned as if in a romantic movie. We embraced and kissed before my husband sat opposite me and we feasted, while anticipating our two-week second honeymoon to other European vistas.

North Wales

On highways leading us to beautiful North Wales, I noticed how much the scenery reminded me of home, of Massachusetts.

"Well, our settlers came from here," George reminded me.

Late in the day, we discovered our destination. St. Beuno's Jesuit Spirituality Centre, which was built as a college in 1848 in the town of St. Asaph. Unlike Gloucester, Massachusetts, which is only thirty miles from a metropolitan area, St. Beuno's seemed remote though it had large and attractive facilities.

I discovered a unique program at St. Beuno's. One member of the Jesuit staff visits a parish for a year and trains a lay minster in Ignatian spiritual direction. At the end of the year the parishioner continues her training at a nearby retreat house, and eventually joins the staff.

We explored North Wales by car, the lanes between the hedges, though charming, was so narrow that our rental car was clipped by another car. "Not a problem," we were told when we returned the car to the rental store. "Happens all the time."

Ireland

After a swift yet stormy ferry ride to Dublin and a train ride to Limerick, we met our dear friends Primm and John ffrench, who had a home in Ireland. They whisked us away to Dingle, the birthplace of my paternal grandmother, Katherine, who had died before my parents married. John drove us down into Dingle with its windy road that led to a magnificent beach.

In the afternoon I visited the parish with its unique statue of Mary, which shows her sitting and reading to two children. The pastor offered to help in finding my ancestors, yet shocked me by saying in the rural region where Katherine was from, those who starved to death during the famine were buried in pits, not in regular graves. Thanks to God, my great-grandfather had got his family to escape.

Paris

After more travels in Ireland, we took a boat, *St. Patrick*, to France. In Paris, we immediately went to the Champs-Élysées, and chomped on chocolate croissants while looking at the Arc de Triomphe. The next day, we visited Notre Dame and Sacré-Cœur, where in a pew I sensed, as many others have, Jesus' face coming directly toward me. Often seekers ask where God is in their life. *I know that God has found us. This brief jaunt is a gift from Her.*

Belgium

Then it was a mad dash for the train off to Belgium, where I was to give a talk at the American College of Louvain for a summer program. After my talk, we were invited to dine with the college president and joined by twenty students from diverse backgrounds, all of us united by faith.

At ten in the evening, George and I sauntered down an ancient street to share glasses of wine in the town square. It was the perfect ending to our pilgrimage. The next morning, it was off to the airport.

On the plane ride home, images flooded me, embracing all the faithful believers, who had in turn embraced me. *I have experienced the true "universal church."*

21

SPIRITUAL LEADER

Massachusetts and Spain, 1991

As soon as we returned from Europe, George's job as the business manager at Labouré College, run by a women's religious order, was suddenly terminated. This meant that we could no longer afford our apartment in Belmont, and had to move to a much smaller place in the adjacent town of Arlington. For a year, George was unemployed and took some courses at Weston. George often commented, "I don't know if they're learning about the real world." His next job was at Cambridge Cares About AIDS, a community-based organization serving people who are living with or at risk of HIV/AIDS.

Shortly after moving to Arlington, I gave the keynote address at a conference sponsored by bishops, in Baltimore, Maryland. I was able to share my experiences from my mission to East Germany. As my topic, I chose to reflect on the courageous actions of Protestants and Catholics in confronting the Soviet dictatorship, to free the people and teach about the oppression of the secret alliance that spied on relatives, friends, and family. The talk wrote itself for the audience, which included attendees from national movements and organizations beyond the parish system.

A Spiritual Journey to Ignatius' Home in Spain

I was not back in the States for long. Because I taught the practicum and because of my ministry in Ignatian spirituality, Weston sponsored my inclusion in a journey, directed by the Paulist professor Thomas Kane, to Spain. Another good friend, John O'Malley, S.J., was adviser for the trip that included a number of Jesuits and laywomen and men.

Loyola, Ignatius' birthplace in northern Spain seemed isolated and attractive, with a retreat house that featured spacious rooms. Looking through the windows, I saw a nearby hill and felt strangely drawn to climb it the next morning, which I did.

With heightened anticipation, I climbed, sensing God might reveal something special to me. What was at the top? I saw six slovenly sheep sprawled on the ground. Very clearly I heard God's voice, "Feed them!"

Afterward, I shared my story with one of the priests, asking, "Do you think that *I'm a sheep*? Do I just follow the herd?"

"God didn't say *you* were a sheep. You were told to minister to them. Cheer up."

On the following morning, despite my awe of being in the town where Ignatius lived, I summoned the courage to go to the home where he was raised. The room where he recovered from his battle wound was arranged just as it had been in 1521. On one side were pews and kneelers where I took a place, knelt, covered my face, and sobbed for a considerable time. No words could be offered. The deep gratitude from my heart spoke in tears.

A few days later, we took a bus south across Spain where we saw fields of magnificent sunflowers, to Barcelona, a superb city where Ignatius studies with grade school children. From there, we spent a night in a nearby Benedictine monastery so high up that some people reach it praying at the altar. It was there that Ignatius finally gave up all elements and signs of being a military man. In a small town nearby, Ignatius had experienced more strong spiritual growth.

Ignatius eventually went to Paris to study for a degree and to gather companions attracted to his spiritual gospel methods. What I particularly cherished was that his spiritual depth and methods came while he was a Catholic lay believer. Traveling to the source of my ministry of spirituality felt recuperative and almost redemptive.

Back home we were celebrating the expansion of our family— Leslie's son Andrew and Tierney's son Ryan, a wonderful surprise, having never had sons ourselves.

As our fortieth wedding anniversary approached, two lay students insisted we celebrate it at Weston. Dixie Burden opened her home on Brattle Street for a party and Robert McCleary planned the tribute. Early on the day of the anniversary, February 27, my phone rang to inform me that due to a blizzard, Weston was closed for the day! But blizzard be damned, the party went on. George and I entered a room crowded with friends, who braved the storm to celebrate us. A message even came from Jim Keegan, S.J., who was in Europe. The ceremony and feasting were enjoyed by all. Our close companions were lay and celibate; celebrating the longevity and faithfulness of our married life with them was the most precious anniversary gift.

But not everyone at Weston was comfortable or understood marriage. One morning one of the faculty priests was waiting for me at my office door. By way of a greeting, he said to me, "You were on television last night, on *The Group*, on WGBH."

"Yes, I was." *Doesn't he know that I have been their spiritual specialist for months now?*

"Virginia, the issue of population control came up and you should have voiced the Church's view against birth control, but you did not. Why did you avoid that Catholic opportunity?"

Maybe because I don't agree with it. Maybe because I've had miscarriages and pregnancies. Maybe because I'm a woman.

Retreats

The ministry I cherished most was how to help believers connect personally to God. The value of a week's retreat is the silence and the time, not only to pray but also to discover where God is in one's life. On an Ignatian retreat, each person is given three scripture readings a day to initiate the process. How God is revealed comes in various ways.

While directing one retreat, I spent an hour or so in the afternoon at Good Harbor Beach, where I saw a man walking toward the parking lot carrying a beach umbrella. Behind him was his wife, tending to the kids and carrying a blanket, a canvas bag bulging with the kids' seaside toys, and a cooler for their refreshment. She looked haggard.

I couldn't get her out of my mind, dreamt of her that night, woke up in the morning with her beside me on my bed. I finally went to the chapel one evening thinking of her, and in the semi-darkness, I heard the message God was trying to impart, "Virginia, you are so over-extended doing my work that I can't get to you."

The same message came through scripture to one of the women I was directing on the retreat. While reading Jeremiah on her own—it was not suggested by me—she came across the story of a she-camel lost frantically in the wilderness, and she knew from that image that God was speaking to her about being over-extended. Ten years later, when writing to me, she said the Jeremiah passage still puts in an appearance.

Retreats, even by the ocean, are not vacations. It takes time to still the mind, to let go of the daily busy-ness of one's life in order to hear God in the quiet of the retreat. Neither the retreatant nor the director knows how God will be revealed, whether in images from the shore, gospel passages, the seagulls screeching as they hunt for fish on the beach, or the sunlight flooding the refectory.

A doctor from Canada had come on retreat and was grieving because his wife had left him for another man and had taken the children with her. The retreatant prayed with the scripture passages I suggested. Nothing happened. He brought his pain directly to God. Nothing happened. Then, one day, sitting on the rocks, staring at the sea, he saw himself tending to a vicious gash on a patient's leg. But, suddenly, he saw someone next to him, helping him. It was Jesus. A great peace came over the retreatant. "The consolation was that my wife had left me, but she had not taken God with her. Or my desire to heal."

During the spring semester of 1991, my focus with my own spiritual director was shifting. He suggested I see in my prayer what image of Church came up and how I fit within that image. Not surprisingly, the image of the Cranwell Chapel in the Berkshires appeared and saddened me. I had recently learned of the destruction of the chapel when a hotel magnate bought the land and bulldozers went to work. One Sunday, George and I drove out to the site and picked up some small chunks of stained glass embedded in the ground near where our beautiful chapel had stood.

Other images came to me. Some of small churches, but the most frequent image was of a very large church, all dark and empty inside, with me standing alone in it. "In no image of a parish church are you doing anything. I find that curious," my director commented.

At the end of May, I decided to retire. Weston's president, Robert Manning, S.J., was lavish with his praise for me at a retirement luncheon given in my honor. On the following Saturday morning, after the movers left with our furniture, George and I got in our car and drove west on the turnpike. George switched on the radio to NPR. I almost didn't believe what I was hearing, a broadcast from St. Peter's Festival in Gloucester. Its unique feature is a dock jutting out over the ocean, which is greased. The townsfolk try to walk to the end of the wharf without falling off into the sea.

In my mind, I saw the greased wharf, but on it were cardinals with red bans on their sleeves, bishops with miters, and priests in Roman collars. They were bumping against each other, slithering, sliding, with arms outstretched, trying to stay on the wharf, but landing in the water. *That's where leadership is right now. They are so confident that they can do <u>without</u> God's people, but the Church is God's people.*

EPILOGUE

In the peaceful Berkshires, I often imagine a map of the United States and reflect on the many graduates from the Weston, of whom I am so fond. Starting in New England, I pray for Mary Beth, who is Director of Pastoral Services at St. Raphael Academy in Rhode Island. Before that she served as a hospice chaplain, a campus minister at Brown University, and led a Catholic adult program for a diocese on Long Island.

In the Midwest, I picture Ginger, who has had a full career. She has been a campus minister, became a Lutheran minister, and headed a parish.

Furthest south in Texas, I envision a couple whom I like to think I was instrumental in arranging their marriage. Glen and Adrianne were both Weston alumni, but had not been there at the same time and had never met. When Adrianne told me she was going to get her doctorate at Theological Union in Berkley, I said, "Look for Glen Ambrose. He is also studying in Berkley and is quite good looking." A few years later, with their advanced degrees and wedding rings, they moved to San Antonio, where they are raising two sons and work in a Catholic college.

In the Midwest, I can visualize three graduates who teach at Notre Dame. In Chicago, I remember Cathy, who for decades has been a pastoral associate in three different urban parishes. Crystal is nearby, as Director of Campus Ministry at University of Dayton.

Further west, from Arizona to Southern California, are alumnae from Weston. All the way north to Seattle. In Denver, are graduates Joe, a teacher in a Jesuit high school, and his wife, Susan, a medical doctor.

These are just a few of the wonderful students I have worked with over the years. Many others write for Catholic publications or serve as missionaries or are parish leaders. Lay ministers all living full, rich lives, and are witnesses to God. But the Vatican must ordain layministers. I cling to the hope that until that day, the Church will stay alive, because unfortunately the Church is falling apart.

Vatican's insistence on celibacy, refusal to ordain women, and their interference with women's bodies correlates to fewer men joining the priesthood, sexual abuse continuing, and attendance at mass dropping significantly.

For many priests celibacy leaves an ache in their heart. A diocesan priest on a 30-day retreat, came to me after four days with tears streaming down his face. He said that he just turned sixty and the only experience he remembered being held for any length of time, was by his mother as a young child. It was also the last he recalled being told that he was loved. He had been a fine priest, cherished by his parishioners, but he felt this awful ache for more than gratitude and respect. That he was able to share his sadness, and even anger with God, gave him some solace.

Parishioners are also suffering and moving out of the Church with their feet and with their voice, because where is the real opportunity for voice or change for the people in the pews ? In the U.S., lay voice can be heard in some Catholic organizations. But, these organizations seldom reach out or pressure local bishops and that is where the power is—where decisions are made for the diocese and beyond.

There are Trappist monks who seldom speak aloud, but pray often; Charismatics who speak in tongues and pray often; and folks who go to Mass, listen to the priest, repeat aloud the liturgical responses, but who seldom speak personally to God.

As I take the time to reflect on the formation of my own faith, I realize that I was enormously blessed to have grown up in two churches. Notre Dame, the French church, had shaped and formed my spirituality. Immaculate Conception, the Irish church, had shaped and formed my Catholic identity. That is why I have been called to discern a difference between the two experiences, even though in each, were elements of the other.

There is a new phrase in America, "I'm spiritual but not religious." Seldom does one hear, "I'm religious but not spiritual." I've never heard anyone declare, "I'm spiritual and religious." Seemingly accepted in the connotation of 'religious' is identification with a denomination, with a church, temple, or mosque. 'Religious' is also associated with tradition, particular rituals, or belief systems. Inherent in 'spirituality' is a sense of an interior life, a willingness to let the Spirit improvise on the immediate reality of a believer's heart, or be open to God's encounter within.

What must not be forgotten, is that God loves us. Jesus came to teach us that. His resurrection happened to teach us that. The Church exists to teach us that, to form us in that trust. Events and relationships in our lives, teach us that.

'Love your neighbor as yourself.' I once gave a homily on Mark Chapter 12, Verse 30-31 focusing on the second half of that missive from Jesus. After the mass, the presiding priest came to me and said that he never really thought about the second part. He observed that, "It's okay to love ourselves. I thought God wanted us to sacrifice ourselves, not love ourselves."

Clarity on these issues came to me, but not until I had lived nearly half a life span. Not until I studied theology at the age, according to St. Augustine, when one is mature enough to embark on theological studies and old enough to reflect on one's youth.

Soon after I began loosing my eyesight, my daughter visited to cheer me up. I thanked Pam for lifting my spirits.

"You have your faith and the spirit within to lift you up, Mom. Where do you see God in your life, now?"

We sat quietly. After a few minutes in silence and thoughtful in prayer, I replied.

"When you were five or six years old and couldn't walk very well because of the brace on your leg, I always wore long skirts, so you could stretch out your small hand and clutch my skirt for balance. Now that I'm old, I sense the Holy Spirit in a long skirt and I reach out to clutch Her skirt, to keep me going."

Made in the USA
Middletown, DE
21 January 2020